POSITIVELY
creative

POSITIVELY
creative

*Harness the magic of a positive mindset
for joyful creative living*

KATE JOHNSTON

Copyright © 2020, Kate Johnston

All rights reserved. No part of this book may be reproduced in any form without permission in writing from the author. Reviewers may quote brief passages in reviews.

Published by Ryebird Books

ISBN: 9781948604918 (paperback)
Library of Congress Control Number: 2020915761

Prepared for Publication by Write|Publish|Sell
Cover Design: Fresh Design
Interior Design: Fresh Design
Editor: Audrey Hodge

for the monsters under my bed

Contents

INTRODUCTION 01

1: The Power of a Positive Creativity Mindset 13
2: Natural Creative Forces. 21
3: Establishing Your Positive Creativity Mindset. 37
4: Living & Working with a Positive Creativity
   Mindset. 49
5: How Community Influences Your Mindset. 69
6: When Fear Steals Joy from Your Creative Life 79
7: Transform Shadows to Opportunities 89
8: Keeping That Star in Sight 103
9: Honoring Your Creativity 121

ACKNOWLEDGMENTS 135
ABOUT THE AUTHOR 137
AUTHOR'S NOTE 139
RECOMMENDED RESOURCES 141

Introduction

"Hitch your wagon to a star."
RALPH WALDO EMERSON

This quote is one of my top ten favorites of all time. I remember when I first read these words and the visual that immediately followed. Within seconds my faith in myself was restored. To me, that quote said, "What the hell are you doing following your dream? You need to be leaping and grabbing on with everything you're made of."

Far too many years passed me by where I thought less of myself, where I lacked self-worth, where I didn't think I was good enough, smart enough, brave enough, or creative enough.

I used to think I had to wait for things to change because I didn't believe I had it in me to change my life myself.

I vividly remember an experience with creative visualization—one that couldn't be explained away by coincidence.

INTRODUCTION

I was reading this amazing book by Ted Andrews, *Animal Speak*, and was particularly entranced by the chapter on feather magic.

It was in the middle of the winter, and I was up late at night reading because I couldn't sleep, and wishing that I had a feather so I could put his ideas into practice. Without an actual feather, I pretended to have one. I sat there on the couch, visualized a feather in my hands, and went through some of Andrews' ideas.

Finally feeling tired, I closed the book and headed upstairs for bed.

On the fourth step of my staircase was a real red feather.

That moment pried open a longing inside me that had been sealed off since I was an adolescent. The longing to be phenomenally happy and confident. To travel around the world and help endangered species. To be rich and famous. To be a bestselling author. To have . . .

Unfortunately, our egos have a way of diminishing our hearts. The minute our hearts announce a dream, our egos reply in pity, "And just how do you think you're going to accomplish that?"

I played around with creative visualization after that feather experience, but I didn't have enough momentum or "evidence" to sustain me. My foremost dream had to do with my creative journey. I'd wanted to be a published author since I was about seven years old and I wrote a story about a good wolf. I had imagined, even as a child, my books lined up on shelves in the library or bookstores, complete with embossed dust jackets.

Over time, this dream grew more and more impossible

in my mind—to the point I told myself I was nowhere near worthy enough to be "that kind of an author." Even though creative visualization started off as fun and exciting, it eventually grew tedious as fewer and fewer instances of "proof" showed up to tell me that, yes indeed, I'm on the right path.

Before long, I let other more important tasks and responsibilities replace what I started believing was fruitless. I was a mom, a caregiver of my own mom, working some part-time jobs, and running the house.

At this particular bend in my life, I wasn't ready to believe that I was worthy of my dreams. I quit writing, telling myself it was for the best, and moved on. Or so I thought.

Little did I know that a seed of hope had been planted. It just needed some extra time and nurturing.

When I was reintroduced to creative visualization, it was through a concept I knew only a little about: Law of Attraction. Someone had told me to watch *The Secret*. Like many other people, I was entranced and excited about the range of possibilities at my fingertips, and it was almost as if an old light that had burned out long ago was reignited.

What you put out to the Universe comes back to you. No way. All this time I figured that my thoughts were a result of the negativity in my life. Things weren't working in my favor, so I started feeling badly about myself. Could it be that it's actually my thoughts that are attracting the negative experiences? Seriously? (I mean, obviously, there are more layers to this—but the basics were all I needed to get excited again.)

The idea that positive thinking and creative visualization could actually manifest good things in your life sounded marvelous. But when I shared my awe with a mentor, she downplayed *The Secret* as being "too simplistic and inappropriate" for people who have "real problems."

To this day, I can feel my hope deflating at her words. I let her disbelief influence my view, and I told myself positive thinking and visualizing would never work for someone like me.

Months later, I stumbled upon a podcast about Law of Attraction and how to integrate it into your life. The podcast served as a nice way to spend my thirty-minute drive between dropping the kids off at school and going to take care of my mom at her house.

The messages and lessons began to sink in.

Once again, the hope that I could still make something of myself, I could still achieve my dream to be a published author, and I could still find at-the-core happiness began to bloom. That seed that had been planted was rooting and growing.

And thriving.

My interest deepened. I found other podcasts and read books and got into meditation and started journaling. But I hovered on the cusp for a bit. On the line between wanting change and afraid I wasn't deserving of change.

Then I found Gabby Bernstein.

Maybe it was the timing or maybe it was Gabby's personality or how Gabby explained how to evolve your spiritual path, but I credit her with my breakthrough. With the help of Gabby's videos on YouTube, and in particular, her book, *The Universe has Your Back*, I broke down and took apart what didn't serve me in my life, explored options for a new way of being, and began to rebuild an inner structure on a foundation of self-love, forgiveness, positivity, self-worth, and belonging.

Anxiety and damagingly low self-confidence had been standard ways of life for me. I grew up in a loving, kind, and giving family, but somehow I struggled with self-image. I never felt emotionally strong or secure with myself, and I avoided taking risks whenever possible.

Part of my healing has involved releasing stories that no longer served me. Where I believed I wasn't capable or courageous or smart, I had to shift my thinking and forge new paths so I could write new stories. Where I believed I didn't belong, wasn't accepted, or wasn't liked, I had to break down that programming and build new systems that would allow me to open up and create healthy relationships or mend existing ones. Where I carried anger, resentment, and blame, I had to find forgiveness (in myself as well as others) and release those toxic emotions, which freed up space to allow in love, happiness, self worth, and confidence.

Breaking down that old programming will be a lifelong process because it's a part of my growth. However, I can say with faith: I am better today than I was yesterday. In fact, this is one of my forgiveness mantras.

Probably the most critical aspect of this inner restructuring has been how I speak to myself and how I treat myself. While losing ourselves in our dreams can make us feel better and give us hope, those dreams have a stronger impact on us if we come at them from a place of strength and positivity and belief. The best way to get to that place is to restructure our inner landscapes.

There are dozens of different methods available to us all to help us relax, refocus, expand, heal, soothe, energize, believe, and vibe happily. There are also dozens of people who can help you discover, trust, and love your true self. I highly recommend that you explore podcasts, books, Ted Talks, YouTube videos, blogs, and self-help groups to find the right combination of teachers, healers, and communities to help you make the pivots you need. At the back of this book, I provide a list of resources to help you continue your positively creative journey.

My dream to be a published author was sacrificed multiple times over the years. The reasons why are too expansive to go into here, but for the purposes of this book it's helpful to know that even dreams we've stomped into nothingness can come back to life—but we have to heal ourselves first.

Einstein said, "We cannot solve our problems with the same thinking we used when we created them."

This means in order to make any kind of change in our external lives, we have to start inside first. With our thoughts and our mindset.

Before I could hope to put my dreams back in the running, I had to do some deep inner work. Healing old wounds, breaking down old programming, unwriting old stories, and planting seeds of faith and belief in myself (and the Universe).

This kind of inner restructuring is lifelong. No one can expect to shift once and be done with it. Those stories we grew up telling ourselves are often on repeat performances hosted by our egos, so it's not unusual to slip up from time to time and talk badly to ourselves.

With a lot of practice, I reached a point in my self-awareness where fear-based thoughts got the boot instead of my dreams. That enormous shift allowed me to gather the courage to make a conscious decision to stay committed to my new way of being. If I slip up, I'll catch myself, pivot, and get back to harnessing the magic for my new positive mindset.

As my new way of being strengthened and evolved, my dreams began to take shape in my reality. Not all at once, and not in the way I might have once hoped, but it turned out that was for the best. The unfolding perfectly aligned with where I was in my creative journey. If all my big dreams had been dumped into my lap while I was still early in my healing process, I wouldn't have been able to handle them.

Did I falter here and there? Did I fail? Did I make mistakes?

Sure. Of course.

Did I ever hit rock bottom again?

Nope.

It's important for us all to accept ourselves as human beings and that we're going to have bad days or hit nasty problems or get entangled with unsavory people. There are things out of our control that we must deal with. That's how we grow.

With growth comes the opportunity to choose again, and return to our new stories of joy, self-belief, creative fulfillment, and prosperity.

However, we trip over ourselves when we hook into those less-than-wonderful situations and let our old stories come back to rule us again. This is a choice we make. We choose to look at a bad situation and make it about that person who wronged us fifteen years ago, or the job we didn't get after graduating college, or how we were abandoned when we were seven . . .

You can get dealt a bad hand and not hit rock bottom. You can get bad news but still stay on track with your positive mindset. You can have a bad day but still manifest the life of your dreams.

The belief system I built is personal to me, based on what I call natural writing forces. In this book, I've swapped out "writing" for "creative" so that those readers who are non-writers can tune in effortlessly and hear the truth that we all have the ability to restructure our inner beings in the way that serves us best.

My positive mindset has made all the difference in my creative and real-world journeys. Not only have I been published, but I also built my own business, healed relationships, restructured my inner landscape, and released old programming that kept me limited for far too long. The dreams I have on the horizon are much healthier, and I'm enjoying the paths to them.

Since embracing this mindset, I'm eager to start my mornings because I know inside of each day there are creative possibilities available to me. There is a beautiful aspect to each portion of my day, so I look forward to the midday rush just as much as downtime in the evening or family time on the weekends. My system of positive thinking is so strong now that it has the power to help pull me out of the downward spiral of fear. I have learned how to catch myself thinking negatively and pivot toward self-love and self-worth.

This book is intended to help you formulate a positive mindset based on the natural creative forces that serve you so you can ignite a creative life that you can enjoy with confidence and passion. Throughout this book, I'll give you methods and strategies so that you can create your own positive belief system and a new life story that will help you reach that star—and many more.

*"When there is no enemy within,
the enemy outside can do you no harm."*

AFRICAN PROVERB

Chapter 1

THE POWER OF A POSITIVE CREATIVITY MINDSET

Every single person on this planet is creative. It manifests differently from one person to the next, and many people aren't even tapped into this aspect of their nature. But creativity is within all of us.

Maybe you're a musician or a gardener or a baker or an athlete. Maybe you love to write, draw, decorate houses, sew, or work with wood. Maybe you run a business, teach, have children, or work for someone else.

Whatever you do for a living or for fun provides opportunities for you to be creative. How you want it to show up in your life is at your whim.

You may feel like you're in a position where beginning or developing or even strengthening a creative life isn't possible. It's easy to feel like that, but you have the power to change how your life operates from one moment to the next.

How a Positive Mindset can Work for You

You've probably been creating for longer than a day, so bear in mind that however long and stringently you've been holding yourself back or limiting yourself is going to be somewhat proportionate to how swiftly and effectively you can launch a positive mindset that you'll stick with.

If you're struggling with writer's block, time management, low inspiration or motivation, lack of support, lack of clarity or focus, or low confidence then that is a result of a negative mindset.

Yes, time management issues fall under mindset because time is made through a combination of our self-discipline, goal setting, and actions that are a direct result of how we feel about our creative journeys.

Yes, lack of support from family, friends, and associates is a result of our negative thinking. Our outer worlds are merely a reflection of our inner worlds. What we believe about ourselves will be shown to us externally.

A positive creativity mindset is the difference between a writer who finishes their projects and a writer who can't finish their projects. It's the difference between an entrepreneur who is able to sign clients and the entrepreneur who struggles with sales. It's the difference between a photographer who is clear with her goal to work for an international publication and a photographer who doesn't quite know how she wants to use her talents.

If you want to write for an audience, start your own business, get your artwork in a gallery, get interviewed by Oprah, or land the job of your dreams, then a positive creativity mindset is absolutely necessary because it will foster long-term creative growth and confidence and skill.

Please keep in mind that I'm focusing on long-term solutions in this book. While many of us may be in need of help or ideas to get us through the short term, we still end up back in our ruts once that quick fix is applied. Changing our stories is a long game, but the reward is worth the patience and perseverance.

That said, you'll see immediate ripples in your life once you start engaging with positivity. The ripples may not be exactly what you were hoping for, but you must trust in the process. Those ripples in your life, just like ripples on the surface of water, will expand with momentum. Soon, the changes you want to see in your life will come forth. But you have to apply yourself faithfully, every day, as often as you can.

A positive creativity mindset is one of the key aspects that make up the groundwork of your new story. If your mindset is not centered on positivity or self-belief, you will struggle throughout your creative journey.

A faulty mindset points to a lack of harmony between your real-world self and your creative self. Some people might refer to this as being out of balance, but I think of balance as making hard shifts from one area to the next to even everything out.

There seems to be a lot of effort to keep things "in balance"—how realistic is it for things to stay balanced one hundred percent of the time? Whereas harmony allows us to be more fluid with our efforts. In truth, we don't need every single aspect of our lives to equal each other or balance each other out.

In other words, we can still create during a chaotic day even if that's not our ideal situation. This is my idea of harmony—a flow of different energies that work together and support each other even in less-than-perfect conditions.

This is why building a positive creativity mindset can be so valuable on our journeys. We can still move forward on our paths even when the odds are stacked against us, even when the kids are home sick from school, and even when our clients complain.

Nurturing Your Mindset

Mindset goes far deeper than our conscious awareness. It's in how we carry ourselves, the person we're "being" throughout the day, and habits we fall into. It's extremely easy to get caught up in an old story that limits us, so a regular practice of nurturing your mindset can literally curtail the negative loop in our heads.

The biggest culprit that stands in our way is fear. Fear of writer's block. Fear of completing the project. Fear of success. Fear of not signing clients. Fear of making a fool of yourself. Fear of not being good enough. And on and on.

This fear is so real that we invent reasons to not create:

- I have piles of laundry.
- Gotta walk the dog.
- I'll write tomorrow.
- I'm exhausted.

- I have to shop for groceries.
- Ideas aren't coming today.
- Ideas are coming, but they suck.
- My business sucks.
- I suck.

Believe it or not, those are fear-based reasons. None of them are worthy (or true) enough to put aside your creative work. Sure, laundry needs to be washed and the dog taken care of, but if you're doing those things instead of creating, rather than working those things around your creativity, then you're giving into your fears.

The best way to combat fear is to create *something* every day. *Something* could be a letter to your aunt, a dream, a sketch, a blog post, free email course, a recipe from scratch, a character outline, captions to old photos, painting a sunset, an exchange of dialogue, a video, your entrepreneur bio, a birdhouse, your back cover blurb, a news article, commenting on a favorite business's social media feed, a travelogue, a prayer, or a wish list to Santa.

By creating something every day, you're establishing a habit, which will allow you to build your skills and grow your knowledge. With increased knowledge and stronger skills, you'll feel sincere joy as you work. Joy helps you grow your confidence and take risks. With more risk-taking, you'll meet people and learn more about the field. Increased networking will bring opportunities knocking on your door. With opportunities, your goals will be accomplished and your dream made reality.

Yes, it all starts with creating something every day.

And you know the single most effective tool to help you begin a daily habit?

Cultivating a positive creativity mindset. Where you want to create. Where you're excited to create—even if you're dealing with a challenging chapter, client, or website.

The process to cultivate a positive creativity mindset will be different from person to person because each one of us has different values, goals, and lifestyles. But the principles behind each aspect are generally the same. As long as you're tapped into your strengths, areas of flexibility, values, goals, and moods, then you can harness the magic of positive thinking for joyful creative living.

"Around here, however, we don't look backward for very long. We keep moving forward, opening new doors, and doing new things, because we're curious and curiosity keeps leading us down new paths."

WALT DISNEY

Chapter 2

NATURAL CREATIVE FORCES

Natural writing forces is a term I came up with when I realized that I was having trouble emulating the strategies of comrades-in-pens to write and complete a book. Again and again, I kept saying to myself "but I'm not like that" or "I have kids, so that won't work for me" or "I do better working this way though" and on and on.

Finally, it occurred to me that while many strategies appealed to me, I always had to tweak them to fit my life situations or my personality traits.

Hence, natural writing forces came to be.

For the purposes of this book, I'm taking the liberty of swapping out "writing" for "creative" so that I can explain this concept on a level that all creatives can relate to. Everyone has a whole system of internal and external "forces" that impact their lives, positively and negatively.

Each person has their own personal system at their disposal. Understanding how one writer gets her work done is helpful because it can spark ideas, but keep in mind that her real-world and creative circumstances allow her to find success that way. That process might not be possible for all writers due to an unsupportive spouse, a paying job, or children at home.

Natural creative forces determine what time of day you prefer to work, why you finish your projects, whether you turn to Facebook when the work isn't going well, and if you let fear stand in your way. Some creative forces serve you; some don't.

The easiest way to explain how creative forces work is to envision an ocean tide. They rise and they fall; they bring chaos and calm. But they're always doing something. Somewhere in the midst is you, the creative, a sea god(dess), and you have to decide how you can work best under the ever-changing conditions.

Internal energies such as confidence, motivation, joy, and fear are influenced by and, in turn, influence external forces such as family, physical health, or household responsibilities.

Examples of various qualities that make up natural creative forces

Habits: meditating before work; studying in coffee shops; exercising before creating; working in your pajamas.

Personality Traits: stubborn; easily distracted; loves to share work; high expectations; eager to learn.

Triggers: a colleague's success; contests; blogging or any kind of social media communication; new business idea.

Moods: high (or low) energy points in the day; fearful; stress/anxiety.

You can manage and modify your natural creative forces to build an effective positive creativity mindset that works exclusively for you.

For instance, once an entrepreneur discovers she gets her best ideas while exercising in the gym, then maybe she could plan to go to the gym anytime she's brainstorming new project plans.

Each creative brings their own personal traits, moods, values, strengths, and energies to their work every day. Some of these forces are beneficial while some aren't. Because no two days are ever the same (and we don't feel the same kinds of moods and energies from one day to the next), the creative must figure out how to manage their system of creative forces for optimal performance.

For example, an interior designer's internal forces could include

- Motivated by classical music
- Short attention span
- Increased energy midday
- Inspiration from Mastermind group
- Overly self-critical

Her external forces could involve

- 9–5 job
- Noisy neighbors
- School vacation
- Disorganized workspace
- Supportive family

All of those examples above can influence creative work. The creative must learn how to manage their own specific system of forces so each individual trait, mood, disruption, and energy can work effectively. Negative patterns could emerge if a creative doesn't tame unruly traits such as a short attention span or disorganization.

Everyone has flaws and strengths in their creative practices. Everyone must deal with gifts and challenges in their schedules and routines. The best and happiest creative people are the ones who learn what their forces are, how to work with them, and where to make adjustments when necessary.

Knowing under what conditions you work best will help you build your positive creativity mindset.

Putting Your Curiosity to Work

Remember that marvelous quote by Walt Disney at the beginning of the chapter? Curiosity is an essential property in a creative's makeup. Curiosity is what you need to lean into anytime you need a creative solution or an answer to a question or to brainstorm for a creative project or to figure out your natural creative forces.

If you haven't truly embraced your curious nature, now is the time to do so. Asking open-ended questions is always a great way to get those juices flowing. Depending on how you work, you may want to record the flow of thoughts as you go so be prepared with some paper and a pen, or a voice recorder app on your phone.

As you acquaint yourself with your natural creative forces, try not to hold any expectations or judgments. This will be difficult, but try to remind yourself you're getting a baseline assessment right now and objective honesty will give you the most accurate information. There will be plenty of time later to modify and refine whatever isn't serving you.

Also, it's helpful to remember that this preparation work is an essential step in terms of productivity. For example, it won't matter how well you can write out a business plan if you can't commit to strong, healthy work-life habits.

Building a course, reading a writing guide, and sitting down to listen to a webinar are all great action steps. However, information isn't useful if you don't know how you can apply it in ways that work for you.

How many times have you started—and stopped—a creative project? Why did you stop? What motivated you to try again? How successful were you the next time around? Why?

See what I mean? One question won't cut it. One angle of assessment won't cut it. If you want to really forge a positive creative journey, then digging deep into your natural creative forces is essential.

Self-Assessment

One of the first things you can start right now is to write your story down.

What do I mean by story? The facts and fiction of your life, in a nutshell. We all have old programming and old stories that we've used as reasons, excuses, or motivations. What is serving you and what isn't?

Your natural creative forces can sometimes be a learned result from something in your past, be a part of your psychological makeup, or they could have evolved based on flawed beliefs. For that reason, sometimes it's hard to know if you're responding to an experience because you were triggered with a childhood memory, or if your response stems from a personality trait.

The good news is that you can reprogram anything you have already learned or believed. So if you've told yourself that you aren't good enough to write a screenplay for Hollywood or to be a painter, guess what?

That changes right now.

Spend some time digging as deep as you can go. This will be an ongoing investigation, and don't be surprised when you think you've dug up all there is to know, only to be waylaid by a new memory six months later. That's just the way we work, and it's best to simply accept it, take the new information into consideration, and move on. Getting frustrated with blurry timelines or contradictory stories from siblings won't help you.

The most important job you have, right now, is to home in on the stuff that you're clearly aware of, whether it benefits or impedes you. Start with what you know.

Once you have a working grasp of your story, start breaking details down into categories:

Habits
Triggers
Values/Morals
Beliefs
Motivations/Passions
Strengths

Challenges
Fears
Personality traits
Outside sources
Purposes

Divide each category into two areas: What is serving me? What is not serving me?

You may find some categories have a lot going on while others might be empty. Some parts of your story may cross two or more categories. No worries, this is normal, and it's even fair to say what you're learning about yourself now could change over time. As we're constantly growing, it makes sense that our actions and responses and what motivates us will change as a result. That's why running regular self-assessments is really helpful.

Your notes are for your use only—you don't need to share them with anyone if you don't want to, so don't hold back on your assessments. The more in touch you are with your foundation and your roots, the more successful you'll be on your journey.

A Creative's Place in This World

In the above list, the final item is "purposes." This particular category deserves its own section in this book.

How do you define "purpose"? Specifically, how do you define your creative purpose? Do you have only one, or many? Why are you a creative? What about creating sets your soul afire? What is the worst thing that could happen if you couldn't nurture your creativity?

Everything anyone does on this beautiful planet of ours always comes down to purpose—our "why." We don't do things for no reason, whether it's a good or a bad thing, there's something that sparks us in the first place.

What sparks you?

Creative journeys can be long, frustrating, defeating, overwhelming, and demoralizing. They can also be rewarding, enlightening, challenging, joyful, and magical.

You get to choose what direction your journey can take. This isn't to say you won't get a bump of overwhelm or frustration along the path toward enlightenment and magic. But embrace that contrast. Light is light because of the darkness, and joy is joy because of the sadness.

Experiencing the rough patches helps us clarify exactly what we're after.

Your Purpose will Evolve as You Evolve

This is important to remember. What you wanted in life when you were ten years old may or may not be the same as what you want now, and it will certainly have different details and characteristics regardless. That's because what you experienced since you were ten years old shaped your values, choices, fears, and desires.

Assess your purpose for both your real-world self and your creative self frequently. I actually do a holistic assessment during the New Moon every month, and I review my purposes. There have been things that I thought were important to me five, even two years ago, that today don't matter at all.

Catching the shift in my purpose has meant I had to redirect my journey in some ways. Often in some surprising ways! Without regularly reviewing my overall vision, where I want to be in the next five, fifteen, twenty-five, or fifty years, then I would have continued on a path that was actually taking me away from my new dreams.

This is extremely helpful for anyone who is feeling stuck in their creative journeys. Maybe you haven't gotten as far as you thought you should have by now. Or maybe you're not feeling the same depth of passion about your creative work like you used to. Or maybe you want to change something about your journey, but you don't know what it is, or even if you should bother.

If any of that sounds familiar, then now is a great time to review your purpose—not just for your creative self but also for your real-world self. Our minds, bodies, and spirits are all connected. What affects your real-world self also affects your creative self.

Why Joy will Never Steer You Wrong

Understanding your true purpose will take some time. Maybe a lot of time, depending on who you are and where you are in your life.

If you don't know your purpose yet, or if you're feeling caught among many possible choices, don't force yourself to come to an answer. That's just going to give you bad information.

But without clarity of purpose, it's easy to feel too confused or unsure of our next steps. So you might choose to do nothing. That's a good short-term solution, but don't do nothing for too long, otherwise fear and self-doubt will set in.

When you're ready to assess your situation, test for joy. Every morning, before you get going on your day, ask yourself

1. *What can I do during my creative time today that will make me happy?*
2. *What sounds like fun to do today?*
3. *How can I spend my time creatively so that I feel good about my decision?*

Joy can never, ever steer you wrong. Be sincere and honest with yourself. Joy is not a factor in self-deceit or self-sabotage. Be careful you're not telling yourself that playing video games instead of painting the mural brings you joy when you're actually avoiding a project that stimulates a bit of fear. What you're feeling isn't joy; it's relief. And that's only going to get you off the hook one or two times before the resulting feelings of guilt or shame kick in.

Here's why joy is a reliable go-to emotion. Joy is a natural stimulant. If we're not feeling joy when we create, then we're not going to try our best or be willing to improve our craft. We're more likely to find fault with our work, self-criticize, and allow anger and frustration to rule the day.

When we follow the feelings of joy, then we know we're headed in the right direction. Joy creates marvelous opportunity to evaluate our purpose as creatives.

Purpose will help you find the edge to create, refine, and feel fulfilled, and help you through pitfalls like poor time management and self-doubt. Your "why" also will help you in a practical sense, to plot your path by means of goals that afford a constant vision.

Use Curiosity to Find Your Purpose

What lights you up? What topics or subject areas do you read about with a thirst to know more? What debates get you on your feet? Where do you feel pulled or fulfilled? What dreams do you recycle?

Your purpose doesn't need to be world-changing, but it does need to feel good to you. It should bring a smile to your face, and it should grow and evolve as you grow and evolve.

Knowing that your purpose can help ground you when life gets out of control, and that it can help re-center you when you've lost your focus, it stands to reason that a purpose should not hinge on what other people might want or expect for you. This isn't about anyone else's happiness or fulfillment except your own. While your purpose may, and likely will, affect others, it's still the driving force in your life. No one gets to steer but you.

My purpose was clear when I made the connection between my passion for writing and my passion to help protect the planet and its wildness. I saw a way I could do both, and anytime I ever felt worried I wasn't doing enough, or being true to myself, all I had to do was bring my focus back to my purpose and start from there. I have no doubts in that space.

I challenge you, when you create, to take into consideration if what you're doing lights you up and drives you forward. When you create, how are you showing up in the world and, at the end of the day, how does it make you feel? Where do you want to make your mark on the world, or at the very least, in your relationships with others and your treatment of yourself? What kinds of ways can you do it?

Never forget: When you create, you're making a difference. Your business helps people. Your art makes people smile. Your songs make people sing. Your writing inspires readers. Creatives touch people a thousand different ways, and when you know why you're out there, shining your light, you'll shine it more powerfully.

Putting Your Natural Creative Forces to Work

Your main objective with your self-assessments is to learn how to release what isn't serving you and to tune in to the aspects that fill you with joy, confidence, self-worth, abundance, creativity—all the good stuff. This is ongoing work that will be lifelong. Just like nurturing your physical body is a daily responsibility, so is nurturing your mindset.

Some days will feel like nothing is happening or that you're having a run of misfortune. That's the time to step it up. Ask yourself what natural creative forces serve you to your highest good. Look at the self-assessments that you've been wisely journaling, and pick a few aspects that are possible to act upon or bring forth that moment.

In addition, you can bolster yourself with some mindfulness tools that are always at your disposal. Add an extra session of creative visualization. Take fifteen minutes and walk in nature, appreciating every little thing you see. Meditate with some positive affirmations. Do more positive actions than you normally fit into your day. Smother that negativity with beautiful thoughts.

And keep recording your self-assessments, keeping them in a safe place. I find this to be hugely helpful when I want to understand those triggers that send me into downward spirals. The more I understand why I fall into negative responses, the better chance I have to eliminate or avoid certain situations. Likewise, when I know the forces in my life that make me feel good, I do what I can to bring more of that into my life.

"Don't dance around the perimeter of the person you want to be. Dive deeply and fully into it."

GABRIELLE BERNSTEIN

Chapter 3

ESTABLISHING YOUR POSITIVE CREATIVITY MINDSET

So how do you get started on your new way of being, especially if you're coming from a place of long-term self-sabotage?

There are hundreds of methods and strategies, but I'll share with you the process that worked for me. Maybe it'll work for you too, but always, always keep in mind that my process is founded on my natural creative forces—those habits, triggers, motivations, strengths, values, and beliefs that are personal to me.

For you to build your best process, it's crucial that you first understand your natural creative forces. Going back to what I suggested in the previous chapter, you want to take the time to journal your story. Evaluate as much as you can that led you to this moment. As you write, you'll notice that your emotions will respond in a certain way—pay attention, because nothing gives you clearer direction than how you feel about something.

Once you divide up all those aspects that serve you and don't, you'll have the raw material to help you get started on your new journey.

Consider making a conscious decision to commit to your new way of being. I wrote mine out like a pledge, signed and dated it, and treated that as my initiation to a fun and fulfilling life.

Next, question your old goals and dreams. I gave myself a few weeks to not think about the things I didn't have, and to not fret over the aspects of myself that held me back. Instead, I looked at my life and figured out what was already working, what was already lighting me up, and what I was loving in the here and now.

I talk later in the book about the power of gratitude and how you can apply it in your daily life. This is an important step that helped me break free from the disappointment and misery of not having the things I wanted and discovering the blessings that were already blooming in my life.

It's easy to forget that we created the life we're already living. Sometimes we get so hung up on the things that we haven't yet achieved that we dismiss the things that are part of our current lives. We created those things—the good, the bad, and the ugly! Understand that if you had the power and magic to create the life you're standing in right this moment, then you have the power and the magic to create anything your heart desires.

Observing your life in the here and now and immersing yourself in gratitude for all your blessings is a crucial foundational step to reprogramming your belief system. You can be, do, and have anything your heart desires. Be grateful for what is in your life now and more of that will flow to you.

The next step you're ready for is to re-envision your future. I made tough decisions about whether or not my old goals and dreams still mattered to me. Some I kept but modified; some I ditched. I took a lot of time to get super-clear on my ultimate vision. I expanded my vision, kind of like "leveling up my dreams." I kept doing this until I saw myself in a life that I knew fit my ultimate purpose. A kind of life where I was aligned with my highest self and taking action on the behalf of others for their greatest good.

Once I was satisfied with my envisioning, I reverse-engineered all the different action steps and paths I could imagine. You'll want to brainstorm all possibilities here—including choices that might feel out of your league.

Don't lose sight of the importance of choosing a goal, path, or action step that brings you joy. I asked myself a trainload of questions about what kind of a person I would need to be in order to accomplish Action Step A or to follow Path D. Above all, I refused to end up on a path of misery and self-sabotage again. As long as joy was part of my daily practice, I was in good shape.

Remain open to unexpected possibility—one of my growth mantras. Just because I didn't expect to live in Hawaii to conduct research for my next book doesn't mean that's not a possible path.

This specific mantra helped me so much when I chose paths or action steps because I'd basically created a mini-life story to get me from Day 1 to Day 60, or from Day 1 to

Day 444. Anything was fair game. This is true for anyone. All of our ideas and imaginings, when written down and explored, create a new story that we can begin living today.

Envisioning your mini-life story can involve as much or as little detail as you want. You'll hear from the manifesting experts that specific details are good to help you conjure a clear image in your mind, but to not attach yourself to those details as though that's the only way your dreams will show up. One way of staying detached from the "how" is to add these words as you visualize your dream: I desire this or something better.

The most important aspect to envisioning your mini-life story (or anything for that matter) is to focus on the emotion and how that vision makes you feel.

Emotions like love, joy, excitement, anticipation, peace, satisfaction, and fulfillment are what you want to aim for, and these emotions all help to build your positive mindset.

Once you start practicing feeling these emotions, based on visions you conjure of your mini-life story, they will flow to you faster and easier until they are your default feelings.

You want to be open to all unexpected possibilities, and this is where it can be really fun and magical—knowing your dream can show up at any point in your life and probably in a way that you didn't expect.

Finally, you want to sort through your natural creative forces and figure out how you can apply what you can to support your new way of being, and how to adjust, modify, or eradicate those qualities that block you creatively.

For example, if one of your challenges is procrastination, then that's a trait you'll want to strictly manage so you can hit your goals in a timely manner. How you decide to manage this particular challenge will depend on you and how you work. Being aware, though, that it's a creative block, is the first step in the process.

Harnessing the magic of positive thinking for a more joyful creative life is a practice that, over time, will become a skill. A lifestyle. To that point, every day you have a marvelous opportunity to strengthen and foster this skill.

When in doubt, breathe. Find a quiet place, get into your rhythm of breathing, and center yourself. Dr. Joe Dispenza says, "When you're in the present moment, you're the most creative." Fretting about the future you fear or getting hung up on the past you regret will not boost creativity. The now, *your now*, is where you have the most power and energy to attract the creative life you desire.

So. When in doubt?

Breathe.

Why Positive Thinking is more Powerful as a Habit

We've all been there. We have a few great days and we're feeling strong, upbeat, and optimistic about things. Life looks marvelous. Beautiful thoughts roll around our minds and the side effect is a happy mood and high-vibe energy.

Then the bad news hits. Maybe you didn't get the promotion. Or you lost a client. Or you didn't make your quarterly financial goal. Or you got another rejection.

Suddenly your outlook on life isn't so sunny. Your mind starts chipping away at all the *whys* and the *how comes* and *if onlys*. Once your mind spirals downward, your entire mood deflates, and your attitude darkens. The negative self-talk escalates in this environment of shadow, and you tumble further into the abyss of self-criticism.

Getting ourselves back to the light isn't difficult, but it requires practice. The easiest way to practice is to rehearse positive thoughts throughout your day even when you're not self-shaming. Make a point of reciting positive thoughts several times throughout the day. Attaching this routine to habits that are already established is most effective, like while you're brushing your teeth or driving to work.

Your recitation of positive thoughts will eventually become a habit and easily accessible in your mind. When you catch yourself thinking negatively, lean into your arsenal of positive thoughts that you've already cultivated. Repeat them over and over until you feel better and the negative self-talk disappears.

There will be those bad days when the negative self-talk goes on and on. If you suddenly realize five hours have passed and all you've been doing is slamming yourself, don't worry. It's never too late to pivot toward your positive mindset. You want to use every opportunity possible to fill your mind with good stuff because this simply strengthens your whole being and can only lead to more good stuff.

You'll likely hit a stretch where you feel like you're ping-ponging between feeling joyful and feeling lousy. This is because your positive mindset is expanding and taking up space once used by limiting beliefs. This is a great sign, even though it can feel like you're getting nowhere or that you've plateaued. You may even feel neutral or indifferent, possibly exhausted.

First of all, remind yourself that you're feeling this way because your inner work is taking off. Here's your chance to ride the momentum.

Second, try to gauge what emotion you're feeling in these moments. Abraham-Hicks, "a group consciousness from the non-physical dimension," teaches on the laws of the Universe, particularly Law of Attraction. Below is an emotional guidance scale based on their teachings:

The Abraham-Hicks Emotional Guidance Scale

Joy/Appreciation/Empowerment/Freedom/Love
Passion
Enthusiasm/Eagerness/Happiness
Positive Expectation/Belief
Optimism
Hopefulness
Contentment
Boredom
Pessimism
Frustration/Irritation/Impatience
Overwhelm
Disappointment
Doubt
Worry
Blame
Discouragement
Anger

Revenge
Hatred/Rage
Jealousy
Insecurity/Guilt/Unworthiness
Fear/Grief/Desperation/Despair/Powerlessness

We want our baseline emotion to be in the high-vibe portion of the spectrum of emotions. The emotion of joy will attract joyful experiences. The emotion of optimism will attract optimistic opportunities.

A positive creativity mindset then, which would be built from emotions like positivity, appreciation, passion, and empowerment, would attract experiences and opportunities that match those vibes you're putting out.

The middle of the scale falls around the Pessimism/Frustration/Overwhelmed area. This is flat, neutral territory that can veer into bad mojo because there is a sense of you getting caught between the push and pull of life. A sense of getting nowhere. Don't give into those thoughts!

When we're in this mode of feeling (or any of the emotions in the lower half of the scale), then you want to slow down, take a deep breath, and turn your attention to a small, bite-sized action step. For now, don't think about the big dreams you're after. It's time for a baby step.

Reach for a fact-based thought, a truth. This is a thought that you'll want to keep in your pocket as kind of an emergency pick-me-up, because you'll be in need of it again.

This type of a thought is grounded in concrete evidence that you can't deny. Everyone will have a different set of fact-based thoughts based on their life experiences.

Some might look like the following:

~ I'm athletic.
~ I'm good at math.
~ Animals like me.
~ I have an amazing best friend who supports me in everything.
~ Children respond positively to me.
~ I make a mean chocolate cake.

Just one thought can grow with detail. Expand this thought with related memories or evidence. Maybe you won the spelling bee in high school, or you got a promotion at work, or you've been complimented on how kind and caring your children are. Keep adding layers so that you create a new story based on this very simple yet powerful truth.

Now you have a beautiful vision you can conjure anytime you hit any of those emotions on the lower half of the emotional guidance scale. You can use this vision when you're already feeling pretty darn good and you want to feel more amazing.

Sometimes it helps to write this vision on an index card and keep it in your purse, or post it in your workspace, or record yourself reading this story out loud and save it on your phone. Or all of the above! There's no way you can overdo this technique, so have fun with it and make it accessible to you any time you need it.

Every day that you live your new way of being, you have a choice: Do I hook into the old stories of limiting beliefs and low self-worth? Or do I open the pages of my new story of positive mojo and self-love?

I've found that each time I choose to focus on my new story, I'm strengthening the habit of positive thinking which leads me to limitless creativity and boundless confidence. That kind of foundation can only help me improve my writing skills, manage my time, stick to my creative projects, and grow my creative business.

Think positively every day, create every day, and feel your life pulse with magic.

"You can start with nothing and out of nothing and out of no way, a way will be made."

MICHAEL BERNARD BECKWITH

Chapter 4

LIVING & WORKING WITH A POSITIVE CREATIVITY MINDSET

I'm a believer in the holistic approach, which is based on the philosophy that the health of our physical bodies is tied to our emotional, psychological, spiritual, and creative well-being. When we neglect any of these aspects, the others are negatively impacted. Conversely, when we nurture one part, the other parts benefit.

In regard to mindset, we must not only focus on the mind. For true joy and confidence and rumbling creativity, we have to incorporate all aspects of our being because of how one affects the other.

The mind (where the ego lives) affects the flow of our spiritual energy. Negative thoughts will slow or block our energy, whereas positive thoughts will increase or enhance our energetic flow. Energy that is gunked-up with negative thoughts can actually make our physical bodies respond with lower vibes like illness, pain, or exhaustion. Spiritual energy filled with positivity can lighten and boost our physical bodies.

You must have a solid understanding of how you work best holistically. You won't be successful building a positive creative life if you're careless with your physical health, for example. This, again, comes down to knowing your natural creative forces. Where do you thrive? Where do you flounder? What aspects are currently undergoing major shifts?

Knowing your strengths, values, habits, triggers and all the other aspects that impact your creative self is the first step. The next step is applying the traits that support you creatively, including how they impact your workspace, time management, project management, and decision-making.

There is no right or wrong way to establish a foundation to your creative life. Choose the way that works best for you. Often, we have to explore several rounds of trial and error before we find a groovy rhythm. To complicate things further, what worked for us six months earlier with project A won't necessarily work for us in our current situation with project D.

Your Creative Spirit Pledge

Ever made an oath to yourself about your commitment to your creative spirit? Writing a statement about how you're going to treat your creative spirit forges a powerful bond between your real-world self and your creative self. This pledge can take the form of bullet-point style declarations, a single sentence, or a letter. Do what feels right to you.

Above all, sign and date your pledge. Put it somewhere that you can access easily. You can even draw up a new pledge however often you feel necessary—every thirty days, once a year, whatever.

This pledge is a promise you're making to your creative spirit. It's a powerful message that vibrates with belief that you can do—you want to do—what you set out to do.

Honoring Your Creativity amid Obligations

One of the most common blocks for people who want to pursue their creative impulses is real-world obligations. We don't feel like we have the right to choose our creativity over making dinner, doing laundry, or playing with our kids. A related issue is when we think we don't have the time to create because we have to go to work so the bills get paid.

In those moments it's easy to forget that creativity is a natural part of us, and when we continually choose to not nurture it, then we're choosing to disregard our health.

We see our situations through a variety of lenses. If we're figuring out our schedule when we're feeling overwhelmed or stressed, then we'll make a choice based on those low-vibe feelings. We'll be less likely to see opportunities for fitting in creativity in what we perceive to be a guardrail-to-guardrail schedule. Making decisions from that state of being will only provide you with a narrow and limited viewpoint.

If you've caught yourself in the middle of making crummy decisions because you're feeling crummy, you can always pivot. Try asking yourself these important questions:

1. What can I do right now that will bring me joy?
2. Which activity between A, B, or C would fulfill me today?
3. How I can turn my day around so that I feel relief?
4. What mindfulness activity can I do for five minutes that will re-center me right now?
5. Am I choosing based on my core values?

Interestingly enough, we tend to be more productive and focused and joyful in our real-world obligations when we honor our creativity. That's because we're holistic beings, and everything we do impacts everything else we do. Treating ourselves with love and care and respect, then, can only encourage growth and progression toward our dreams.

Creative Space

Even if you don't work from home, it's nice to have a place that is sacred to your creativity. A place where your creative self dwells, creates, and produces. Your creative spirit needs to be in an emotional and physical space where it can thrive. This space is also your creative spirit's sanctuary. A safe place to retreat, heal, replenish your resources, tap into your natural creative forces, and reflect.

Because of the holistic nature of our beings, a healthy and thriving and safe creative space will impact our inspiration, ideas, confidence, and time management in positive ways. When you think of your workspace as your creative spirit's habitat, then you're more likely to take good care of it.

Claiming our own personal space for our creativity is important, but it's not always easy or possible. Many moons ago, my writing space was given up for a nursery and I was forced to share our refinished basement in our tiny ranch home with my husband. This was an utter failure as we have two different working styles. He chit-chats, drums his fingers to music, and shuffles paper noisily, compared to my need for quiet (or wordless music) to support my focus and concentration.

I learned quickly that I need my own creative space, but until then I was forced to share a room with Hubs. When we started looking for a bigger house, one of my requirements was my own study with a door I can close. I pretty much manifested a sweet work-at-home situation based on what I learned about myself and my natural writing forces.

Not all of us have the luxury of our own creative space, and I sympathize if that's you. If you live with other people you're subjected to their habits, temperaments, and schedules—which will impact your creativity output.

But let's face it: you probably can shower in privacy. Why can't you create in privacy?

Again, creativity is a natural part of us and it needs nurturing and care like every other part about us. But it's up to you to set boundaries.

If there's no actual space for your creative work, for example, another room that you can claim, then you have to ask for a common room all to yourself during a set period of time. This will help you establish two important factors at once: workspace and time management. The people you live with are more likely to fall into a routine of giving you space because they'll be able to plan around your schedule.

Additionally, asking other people to make accommodations for your schedule will encourage you to follow through.

For example if you can ask for the kitchen table between 9-10 pm, then family members/roommates know to move to another room.

Perhaps you have a basement or a garage that is currently filled with junk or equipment. Can you clear out a corner large enough for a desk and chair?

Are you able to swap family tasks with your significant other? If one person cooks, the other person does dishes—the task you're not responsible for is your creating time. If there are children involved, swap bedtime routines every other night or do a split shift—wherever you're not required is your opportunity to create.

Tools & Equipment

Depending on your area of creative focus, your arsenal may be sparse or quite complex. Speaking as a writer, I can make do with a limited number of tools and still accomplish a wide range of tasks. If you're a business owner, you probably need access to much more than a pen, notebook, and a laptop in order to fulfill your creative needs.

For the purposes of this book, though, we want to focus on establishing an inspirational and functional workspace that calls to your creative spirit so that you can build a joyful creative life.

~ Assess your current space and write down what you need, what doesn't suit your purposes, or anything you'd like to modify.

~ Start a running list of equipment and resource material that you'd like to add to your space.

~ Browse online and in stores in your local area, and choose material that makes you happy and excited.

~ Ask colleagues what tools they like to use and why—this is to inspire you with ideas and supply you with information, not necessarily to encourage you to do what someone else does.

~ Is there anything you'd like in your arsenal that you can't afford, can't find room for, or feels more indulgent than practical? Can you save up money for it, ask for it as a birthday present, or plan to incorporate it later in your journey? Start a running wish list and tack it up somewhere in your space. Make a promise to treat yourself to an item on your list when you reach a specific creative goal.

~ Assemble a portable creativity bag. Keep this ready at all times. This will allow you to create at places outside of your regular workspace.

Caring for Your Space

Every year, twice a year, I reserve one full weekend to clean, organize, decorate, and enhance my study. When possible, I choose to align what I call "nesting" with the New Moon because of its replenishing energy.

It's one of my favorite things to do, and I go all in. I clean out folders, transpose old notes into my scrap writing notebook, throw things away, refresh any inspirational notes or quotes on my walls, get new candles. I play some of my favorite music while I do this work, and I always do something new to my space.

This is the only place in my house where I can work totally under my own terms, so it's up to me to take care of it. Cleaning, organizing, and *prettifying* my study honors my creative spirit. Here is my opportunity to fortify my purpose: *Why am I a writer?*

~ Take some time to construct your workspace if you don't have one established. Be intentional and enjoy the experience.

~ If you have a work area, schedule some time to clean, organize, and personalize it.

~ If you're forced to use common space in your home as your creative area, see about decorating it with artwork, plants, salt lamps, or anything else that will serve as inspiration and will also be enjoyed by the other people you live with.

~ Connect to your purpose through your workspace. Journal through this experience. Answer this important question: *I am a creative because* _____ *and my workspace will help me to achieve* _____. *This is why my workspace is also sacred space.*

~ Snap a photo of your finished space and show it to a supportive friend or family member as a way of fortifying this important milestone. Add your photo to your journal and write about how this action step makes you feel.

Time Management

I believe in the importance of creating every day for a minimum of fifteen minutes. I don't think you have to work on your current project for this fifteen-minute session to count.

You can edit your website, add to your Discovery notes on your characters, practice a new Instagram feature, add photos to a blog post, make Pinterest templates.

Your creativity is always flowing, whether you feel it or not. The more you tap into it the more it will flow for you the way you want it to. Honoring your creative spirit on a daily basis is akin to feeding your physical body on a daily basis—you're aiding in its growth and health.

Most people don't create every day unless it's a paying gig. I find this sad. Seems like we're more willing to sacrifice the privilege of creating for the problems or needs of someone else, like cooking a meal for the family, getting swept up in a heated debate on Facebook, or listening to a friend complain about her husband. And don't get me started on how often people choose to watch television or play video games or scroll through emails and social media instead of sitting down to create.

Keep in mind I'm speaking generally, and there may be legitimate issues that are standing in the way between you and your creative project. The issues I stated above are actually quite easy to fix because it's a matter of making a different choice. To find creative solutions for issues that are much more serious in nature (for example, taking care of a loved one who is ill) will take a bit more inner work.

Once we understand that maintaining creativity is just as healthy for us as maintaining proper sleep and nutrition we're more likely to find a window of time every day to create.

Time Management as a Mindset Issue

I believe that if you want to make forward progress on your creative journey then you need to treat your creative work like a job. Scheduling your creative sessions in a calendar and refusing to open your office door when your spouse knocks are just a couple of boundaries you could implement if you want to guard your time and space.

Because we all have the same number of hours in a day, the difference between one creative and another (in the sense of time) is how we spend our minutes. Most of us waste precious minutes here and there doing non-essential tasks like scrolling through social media or taking an extra-long shower.

I feel safe to say that everyone has some clump of time to create every day—some of you may have to look very hard for that clump, but it's there. Before I ruffle too many feathers—I concede there are *those days* where we just can't get our creative work in. I get it. So, if "every day" is pushing it, then let's say "regular basis"—a schedule that's consistent and can easily become a habit because you're tending to it often enough.

In addition to frequency, you need to consider duration. How long of a period of time you can devote in one session. Some creatives can invest a couple of hours, while others can only squeeze in twenty minutes per session.

One creative does not have an advantage over the other just because they can work more frequently or for longer periods of time. Sure, maybe they'll log in more work on average but that's only a small part of the extremely big picture that is the creative journey. As long as you're honoring your commitment in the way that best fits your natural creative forces, you can't go wrong.

For those who want to increase the length of time you create, first develop a solid habit of tending to your creativity every day (regular basis). This is the building block. When you're ready to increase your duration, refer to your natural creative forces in the sense of understanding and managing circumstances that won't lead you to self-sabotage.

Whether or not you commit to a habit is all mindset. Sure, habits are vulnerable to circumstances and people out of your control—but how you flow from day to day (or, even, moment to moment) comes down to your mindset.

1. What do you want to accomplish in regard to your time?
2. Why is this important to you?
3. What choices do you have to accomplish your goals regarding time?
4. Where you feel stuck or limited, brainstorm alternatives that may require outside help or extra resources and list them.
5. How will you design your day to fit your goals? How will you design your week to fit your goals?

Once you get going on your daily (regular) creativity habit, record your progress. If you find that you self-sabotage repeatedly, assess the reasons why.

1. What are you allowing to interfere or distract?
2. What's your internal monologue?
3. What belief systems are getting in the way?

A productivity hack

We tend to think of progress and productivity in terms of time, but if you already struggle with time management then you're basically paddling upstream. Focusing on a *time-based* routine may not be the most logical approach.

Think of progress and productivity in terms of quality rather than quantity.

Don't focus on duration or frequency. Rather, focus on a creativity-based task within your project.

For example, if you're writing a science fiction novel then decide upon a creativity-based task in regard to a character, a scene, or a dialogue exchange. Every time you get ready for your writing session, erase any thoughts about how long you can actually work and instead concentrate on your creative goal within that project.

This may feel cumbersome at first, because we're so accustomed to measuring our progress by time. You have to remember that any chance we actually create is progress in and of itself because creativity is ever-evolving. It's always changing, growing, and providing new opportunities for us. This is unrelated to time, either frequency or duration. You make progress each and every moment you work, because the more you tap into your creative impulses the deeper of a trusting connection you forge to your creative spirit.

A deeper connection of trust almost always guarantees a smooth flow of creativity whenever we seek it out, which leads to productivity. This goes far beyond time invested. Productivity, at its essence, is an expansion and deepening of your creative experiences. Focus on the task at hand, care for the resulting quality of one's work, and comprehension of the ultimate goals and why all play a part in the joyful and productive flow of creativity.

Suit Up and Show Up

Getting yourself to actually sit down and work is a common struggle among creatives—especially if you're accountable only to yourself. Whether or not you can make it to the computer or to the stack of paper on your desk hinges on your energy levels. If you're exhausted, it might be more difficult to feel motivated to do anything other than the barest essentials.

There's no magic spell here, I'm afraid, other than your own willpower (which, personally, I think is magical in its own right).

- ~ Remind yourself that you need to treat your creativity like a job.
- ~ Remind yourself of your pledge to your creative spirit.
- ~ Remind yourself of your Big Dream.
- ~ Remind yourself that you're the only one who can hitch up your wagon.

Repetitive affirmations centered on motivation can work wonders as well. For example, you have an opportunity to work (kids are in bed, and the house is nice and quiet) but you're lacking interest in your project.

Pay attention to what you're telling yourself in these moments:

~ I'm too tired.
~ I'd love to veg out on the couch and watch a movie.
~ The guys called and wanna go out tonight.
~ I want to go to bed.
~ If I go to bed early, maybe I'll get up early and I can work then.
~ I worked yesterday, so it's cool if I skip today.
~ I have too many other things to do.
~ The weather is perfect for hanging on the beach today.

Do any of these sound familiar? These are just a few examples of how we can talk ourselves out of doing something that feels too difficult or unenjoyable. They all carry creative blocks of fear, limiting beliefs, avoidance, or resistance—no matter how we serve them up.

Even when we soften the blow to our Muse by offering a concession, like doing the creative work at another time of day, keeps us down. Switching things like that—for reasons based in laziness or avoidance—still sends a negative message.

We justify not working because we're socializing with friends or spending time outside instead. While those pastimes are equally important as honoring our creativity, they aren't replacements. When we skip creativity for something else, we end up feeling guilty.

If you hear yourself saying anything like the above, then you're in a position of making a choice: Will I or won't I create right now? Tread carefully, friend. Assuming you're reading this book because you want to create and you want to build a positive mindset that gets you creating effortlessly, then let's get you climbing your way toward *I choose to create right now.*

Come up with a list of ten or so motivational affirmations, personal to you, that you can put on repeat to help you flip from avoidance to taking control of your creative life.

Here are a few that can get you started:

~ I'm honoring my creative self in this moment.
~ Right now, I choose creativity.
~ I'm a creative machine and nothing will stop me.
~ I will feel so proud of myself if I choose to create right now.
~ This is my time to create and I'm blessed to have this opportunity.
~ I'm excited to accomplish a task tonight.
~ I'm honoring my commitment by showing up, no matter how I feel.
~ Once I get going, I'll drum up the energy I need for this task.
~ Doing this will make me feel good about myself.

The above is a sample of my personal running list of affirmations that I use anytime I start to make an excuse that might take me away from my writing time.

Once the negative thoughts hit me, such as "I don't feel like working on my novel today" then I catch myself, take a few deep breaths to re-center, and remind myself what this specific time is for.

Depending on how low-vibe I'm feeling, a string of affirmations may be all I need, or I may need to climb my way through what I call a progressive belief interlude. This is a series of positive-based statements designed to gradually carry me from low-vibe to (at the very least) a willingness to see my commitment through.

These statements build on each other, like a story. For example:

Limiting belief:

I have no energy to work on my website tonight.

Progressive belief interlude:

I may not have energy right now, but imagine how good I'll feel if I just put in twenty minutes. I can focus on my About page, not the entire site, and I won't be overwhelmed.

The issue with the About page is it needs to be updated, so I'll make a list of my most recent experiences. I'll only focus on five, and expand on those with really nice detail. I'll be happy when it's done and I can check it off my to-do list with a big smiley face sticker!

Then I'll further reward myself with a small glass of wine and a book before bed.

Assess Your Circumstances Regularly

Stay connected to your actions and responses and how you feel at the end of the day. This is the easiest strategy to take when you're overwhelmed, uncertain, or transitioning.

1. What strengths have I been able to rely on this week?
2. What triggering events have been setting me off lately?
3. Did I recently get into an argument with a family member or a friend? Did we ever work things out?
4. How has my sleep been recently?
5. Am I worried about anything in particular?
6. Who in my life has really been helpful and supportive lately?
7. Have I been able to stay consistent with my intentions and goals? In what ways have I struggled?
8. What is something new that has flowed into my life lately and how am I handling it?

Don't be afraid to mix things up when you're feeling like you've hit a wall or things are feeling stale. If you couldn't nail down a consistent creativity session six months ago and you gave up, maybe now is a good time to try again.

Always remember that creativity is ever-evolving and so are you. What you thought was a strength two years ago may suddenly hamstring you now. Those triggers that set you off with your last project are non-existent with your current project. A baby in the house has finally taught you the value of responsibility and self-care—two values that have always escaped you, and now you can put them to work in your creative life.

Running an assessment—regularly—on your natural creative forces will help you stay on top of your game. You need to know what's working and why it works so that you can use those attributes to your fullest potential.

"Who you choose to walk and grow with is a major part of life; may they lift you up in hard times, rejuvenate you when you are tired, and remind you of how powerful you truly are."

YUNG PUEBLO

Chapter 5

HOW COMMUNITY INFLUENCES YOUR MINDSET

Whether you live alone or with others, whether you're cruising solo on your journey or you socialize with fellow creatives—your community has the power to support or derail you.

Setting boundaries that guard your creative space, time, and creativity mojo is up to you, and you're the one who has to enforce them. This can get sticky where close family or friends are concerned, so it's important to be crystal clear about your creative goals.

Creative-oriented people are solitary creatures, but humans are social animals. This is why a strong connection between our real world and creative selves is crucial. The creator in us needs to have personal space and time that are respected by others. However, the social part can boost creativity in surprising ways—as long as it's a healthy connection.

Choosing an outpost where you can socialize along your journey comes down to your specific, individual needs. Everyone will seek out different kinds of people, feedback, resources, information, and accountability.

Regardless—finding a hive/team/group/community (whatever you want to call your peeps) is vital to your overall happiness, confidence, and positivity.

Giving back to your support system is just as important as drawing sustenance from it. This is how communities thrive in the real world, and the same is true through a creative community. You'll see that noise and high activity aren't necessarily indicators of a thriving community. Rather, the best, most fruitful communities are founded upon kindness, generosity, and a willingness to listen, learn, and help.

If you live with other people, then your space and time are at risk for interruptions. It's important to have conversations with your family or roommates so that they understand your expectations. Don't enforce unreasonable demands upon your mates. Compromise is key here.

Unfortunately, not everyone in your community will be on board. Have you ever hung out with friends and you start feeling badly about yourself and your lack of success? Or feel silly or small when you talk about your latest project? Did you let that bother you to the point where you began to get down on your own creative life?

"Ignore those that make you fearful and sad, that degrade you back towards disease and death." Rumi

In the creative sense, this means before you allow low-vibe feelings to negatively impact your work, be sure you're not allowing the projections of others to muddy your path.

We tend to overlook the fact that, in many ways, we're influenced by our environment. If you're not thriving creatively, be sure to examine your home life, work life, social circles, and relationships across the board. Who in your life is holding you back or limiting you? Who in your life is not fully supportive? Who in your life makes you feel like you don't deserve your success?

This isn't the blame game. I'm not suggesting our struggles are always a result of someone else's limiting views or opinions. In the end, how we handle every single situation comes down to our behavior and attitude. We must own our self-talk. We must own our self-belief system. No one—not even the most jealous colleague—can make us talk badly to ourselves. However, you also don't want to be associating with people who constantly bring you down.

Remove from your life anyone who's contributing to your limiting beliefs. You don't need to tolerate or socialize with anyone who isn't hoisting you on their shoulders and singing your praises. (And for those who are shouting your name from the rooftops, be sure you're giving them beautiful support in return.)

A strong healthy community (family, friends, fans, colleagues, social media followers) is creative fuel. Next to your own confidence, the rallying cries of people who believe in you are an instant energizer. Surround yourself with people who are strong, generously minded, creatively healthy, and positive and you're more likely to be successful, confident, and joyful.

THE DANGERS OF THE JUDGMENT ZONE

When we compare ourselves to fellow creatives, we're in the Judgment Zone. When we criticize ourselves, we're in the Judgment Zone. Anytime we measure our worth or progress or success against anything outside of ourselves, we're in the Judgment Zone.

The Judgment Zone kills positivity flat out. It takes no prisoners. When we're in the confines of the Judgment Zone, we lose all sense of what's truly important and instead become focused on things that validate our old programming and our old stories.

One of the ways we cast judgment upon others (and ultimately against ourselves) is through jealousy. We fail to be happy for people who seem to be more successful or farther along their journeys; we condemn instead.

If we flipped our jealousy to excitement, we could view those people and their positive experiences as proof that success and happiness and wealth and health are indeed possible.

~ If she can run a successful business, then so can I.
~ If he can find a literary agent, then so can I.
~ If she can go back to school and get her degree, then so can I.

Seeing "proof" of possibility through the success and joy of other people will help you build a positive creativity mindset. You can find evidence all over the place—on social media, in your community, among your friends—and use that as signs from the Universe that you're on the right path, heading in the right direction.

At the core of this mindset shift is the understanding that there's enough in this world to go around. There aren't "only so many" clients out there or "only so many" publishing contracts available or "only so many" galleries that will display artwork.

If we believe in lack, then we'll see lack reflected to us. If we look at colleagues as competition rather than as path-pavers, then we'll feel jealousy, desperation, and failure.

Try this exercise: Think of one person in your field who seems to be more successful than you, or who seems to have more wealth or joy than you. Try to pick someone that has drummed up feelings of envy for you in the past.

Practice flipping your thoughts and emotions around this person so that you're sending them love, acceptance, and support.

One fun game is to picture both of you at a cocktail party or a seaside picnic, and you're engaging in a conversation. Come up with a dialogue exchange where you're congratulating this person and honoring this person for their achievements, and they're complimenting you in return. Have them list out the reasons they believe you're successful. If you find yourself making up accomplishments or pretending you've achieved something when you really haven't, don't stop yourself. Go with it.

Not only will this exercise help soothe the green-eyed monster, but it will also act as a visualization technique where you can call forth feelings of excitement and happiness regarding your dreams.

Establishing Energy Boundaries

Have you ever left a social gathering feeling drained or depressed or frustrated? Introvert/Extrovert discussion aside, no matter what type of personality you have, it's possible to be impacted by the energy of other people simply by less than optimal interactions.

I had a college roommate who suffered from bulimarexia. This eating disorder infiltrated not just her personal life but also her relationships with people.

As the person who saw her the most often, I was her sole support and confidante. I was the one who made excuses for her long absences directly after meals. I was the one who cleaned the room after the binge eating and patrolled the hallway outside the bathroom. All of this intermingled with my pleas for her to get help, to talk to a professional, and to tell her mom.

After a few weeks of dealing with her depression, her lies to her family and friends, and her destructive patterns, I began to suffer from acute anxiety, migraines, insomnia, and loss of appetite.

She switched schools midway through second semester. Two days later, I got a new roommate who had no body image or health issues at all. She was a serious student who had a full-time job to pay for college. We got along great. Within a couple of weeks, I was back to sleeping soundly, eating normally, and my nerves were no longer frayed.

My mistake with my first roommate was that I hadn't guarded my energy. As a "people pleaser" I tended to sacrifice my well-being for the desires of others, which often led to me feeling not so wonderful, more than once. A lot of not-so-wonderfuls built up into a toxic environment.

Guarding my energy or establishing energy boundaries or choosing my well-being weren't things I ever knew to do until I started deep inner work—over twenty years later.

Once I learned how to set boundaries to protect my real-world self's energy, it occurred to me that this was exactly what I needed to do with my creative space and time. Suddenly, a new world opened up to me as I began to realize how much freedom and power actually exist when we protect and honor our creative spirits.

Ironic when you think about it—freedom generated from setting boundaries. I think what happens here is that when we feel safe, we're more willing to explore, step outside our comfort zones, and take risks.

We have faith that all is well.

As long as we're guarding our energy, we can do anything with ease.

"The cave you fear to enter holds the treasure you seek."

JOSEPH CAMPBELL

Chapter 6

WHEN FEAR STEALS JOY FROM YOUR CREATIVE LIFE

When you first decided you wanted to follow a creative journey, more than likely you were motivated by joy. You probably enjoyed conjuring stories. Enjoyed being struck by inspiration. Enjoyed shopping trips to buy supplies for your creative business. Enjoyed learning from mentors, taking workshops, and applying your knowledge. Enjoyed entertaining, inspiring, or teaching other people.

Creativity might have felt like an adventure to be taken on. You likely loved the feeling of putting your ideas into form, probably adored the blank canvas, and loved exploring and challenging yourself to try new things. Inspiration was your fuel, and creation was your passion.

At some point, though, most of us hit a wall and the joy isn't quite so, well, joyful. Joy might even feel like a bad joke after the forty-fourth rejection or a negative write-up in the paper or an irate client.

Bad days are part of the human experience, so we have to be prepared to accept them as a lesson we can learn from, or as an opportunity to grow. From there, as long as our creative spirits are healthy, we can shake it off and get back into the game relatively fast.

However, if joy remains elusive, if we stay down, if we're unable to pull out of that miserable feeling, then that's a red flag.

Sometimes, creatives will continue to work despite the low-vibe emotions. If this is you, proceed with caution. If you force the creativity when you're not feeling the beautiful rush, then the quality of your work and the level of your output could be impacted negatively.

A better approach is to set aside whatever you're working on and address the root cause of your joylessness. Catching it sooner rather than later is beneficial because you're eliminating variables that could muddy your perception.

Generally speaking, fear is the culprit here. Fear can attack in a lot of forms, often manifesting as stress, overwhelm, procrastination, avoidance, self-criticism, judgment, shame, laziness, sadness, exhaustion, lack of interest, defensiveness, frustration, anger, lack of motivation, feeling stuck, negativity, and separation.

Take the opportunity to get real with your creative spirit. If you're perceiving the problem from a place of fear, such as avoidance, then you're not going to find appropriate solutions, because you're already blocking yourself.

For example, maybe you hear yourself saying things like:

"Why are things always so hard for me?"

"Why do bad things always happen to me?"

"There's no way I'm smart enough to figure this out."

"I don't have time for this shit!"

"How could I have thought I'd be successful at this?"

"I never should have taken this risk."

It's okay and totally understandable if you've uttered anything close to the above. We all have! The issue with statements like that means you're approaching your problem from the place of a problem.

If you flip your mindset around, speak to yourself with more belief, confidence, and love, then you'll be approaching your problem from the place of a solution.

Try this exercise:

~ Record the WHAT/WHO and WHEN (all factual data that would be difficult to dispute).

~ Assess your body language and/or emotional responses to the event. Do you have stomach pain? Are you shaky? Can you concentrate?

~ Record, as honestly as possible, what your body is telling you. Obviously, the range for error here can be quite large for those who aren't comfortable tapping into their emotions. With practice, though, you can become quite good at it.

~ Once you have a sense of your emotional state, start asking yourself **why** you think you're dealing with Problem X. Allow yourself to explore all possible reasons, and pay attention to your thoughts and emotions as you do this.

Remember, you're dealing with fear, even though it may have disguised itself as procrastination or as self-criticism. Your fear will revolt under your scrutiny, and you need to pay close attention.

~ Design positive statements based on what you learned about why you're struggling, and use them instead of the negative self-talk.

For example:

~ Instead of "Why are things always so hard for me?"
Say "I am ready to take on a challenge."

~ Instead of "Why do bad things always happen to me?"
Say "I can learn something valuable from this experience."

~ Instead of "There's no way I'm smart enough to figure this out."
Say "I have figured out a problem like this before (cite evidence), so I know I can figure this one out."

~ Instead of "I don't have time for this shit!"
Say "I will do my best to handle this situation, and I can ask for help from (trusted friend or family member).

~ Instead of "How could I have thought I'd be successful at this?"
Say "The fact I even tried is proof of my strength, courage, and self-confidence."

~ Instead of "I never should have taken this risk."
Say "I'm glad that I gave myself the opportunity to try and now I know more than what I knew before."

Do you see the power shift when we swap from negative to positive self-talk? Obviously, these are generic examples but you can personalize them with direct evidence and specific language that hits home for you. Doing a bit of journaling to understand the emotional struggles at play will help you formulate strong positive statements that are meaningful to you.

Exercises like this help you learn about your natural creative forces. What triggers you? What situations do you tend to avoid? What are your limits? For what reason will you break promises to yourself? Under what circumstances will you go all out?

You may or may not get the concrete answers you're looking for in one attempt, but that's okay. You're still gaining self-awareness. You're still strengthening your connection between your creative and real-world selves.

With practice, you can learn to become self-aware so that you'll be able to pick up on external and internal cues more easily.

Eventually you'll be able to outline a relatively objective scenario that can give you some insight as to how to come at your problems through creative solutions.

How Does Fear Play a Role for You?

Fear is an indicator that you aren't in tune with your true self. Sometimes the fix can be as simple as taking a nap. Other times you may need a helping hand. Assess who in your life has your best interests at heart and reach out to them. How can they help you regain ease and flow in your creative and real-world lives?

Keep in mind that fear can be handy. It tells us that we deeply want or care about something. Fear lets us know that we're about to work hard and we're about to take some hits. But we're in trouble when we let fear control us. When we halt our quests because we're too scared of what might happen or what might not happen.

Fear is a problem if it makes us stop believing in ourselves.

The worst response to fear is fear. When we allow it to stop us from pursuing our creativity then we've forgotten our power.

Sometimes it helps to just get real with whatever is triggering feelings of fear. Journaling is one of the most effective methods because it allows you to purge the blocks so positive energy can flow through you.

1. What are your fears associated with creating?
2. What do you enjoy most about your creativity sessions?
3. How quickly does inspiration hit you? How often do you respond? When you respond, what emotions arise?
4. At the end of your creativity sessions, how do you feel about the work you did?
5. When you're not actively creating but you're thinking about it, what feelings come up for you?
6. List all the things in your creative life you consider a win.

7. How often do you step outside your comfort zone in your creative life? What was that experience like?

Add questions and discussion points as you like. The objective here is to contend with fear in a way that makes it approachable. When you can talk about your fear, then you're in the act of taking back your power.

For every fear you have, list a positive mantra that can counteract it. Write them down and keep them someplace easily accessible. Get in the habit of reciting a mantra every time fear stops you from taking action. Then, take the action. Be sure to record the experience afterward.

Fear may be able to grip you by the shoulders, but it doesn't have to shake the life out of you. Summon your positive thoughts, the beautiful things that make you smile, the dreams that motivate you, and chase the fear away.

The power you find within yourself to chase the fear away harkens back to your natural creative forces. Ask yourself what attributes and traits naturally lead you to feeling self-assured and in control.

Remember that your strengths are at their most effective when you're taking care of yourself, both inside and out.

Some self-care tips:
Get more sleep
Eat nutritious foods
Laugh

Help a neighbor or someone in need

Meditate

Buy some indoor plants

Drink more water

Indulge in a hobby

Feed the birds

Smile

Cut down on time spent with negative people

Donate old clothes

Take a friend out for coffee

Journal or find another outlet to release emotions

Spend time in nature

Cuddle with a pet

Exercise

Go to the movies

Surprise someone

Bake

Organize a room in your house

Get a massage or a manicure

Read

Weed your garden

Call up a friend or a family member

*"We don't see things as they are,
we see them as we are."*

ANAIS NIN

Chapter 7

TRANSFORM SHADOWS TO OPPORTUNITIES

The morning is a murky blue-black. The snow-covered ground shimmers under the moonlight. I'm awake at my usual hour but having trouble writing. I take my coffee to the window and study the crooked silhouette of the apple tree, its branches shattered by the storm.

In the yard, I see movement—stealthy and slow; three deer are grazing the barren bushes. I think about the book I'm supposed to be writing, but I'm more interested in watching deer tread cautiously at the edge of dawn.

My writing is suffering. The ideas are there, but, like the deer in the yard, they hover with each step. Wary, nervous, and ready to flee at the first hint of danger.

I'm experiencing a writing crisis—no desire to work on my latest project. I have my coffee and my 4 a.m. writing session all to myself, yet feel no pull toward my study. How did this happen? How could a lover of words, home-brewer of stories, not want to write?

Fear.

As I look out the window, at the deer picking their way across the snow, I wonder about the fears they have to face. Yet, they're still out there—vulnerable but determined. They aren't hiding or cowering.

Quite simply, there are some things we have to do. Deer must eat. Writers must write.

While courage might be the expected or the obvious go-to emotion to battle fear, sometimes we need to go one step further if we not only want to fight fear but we want to stop believing its message.

Most of my creative life I struggled. I usually had no problem coming up with ideas or turning them into novels—I embraced the creating part of the craft. The trouble began when I started sharing my work. It was a disaster. I allowed rejections and negative feedback to shape my perceptions to the point I believed that I'm not a good writer. From that belief, I constructed an entire story that kept me limited and withdrawn and that led me to sabotaging my creative life.

This flawed belief lasted years. Years. And although I wrote (and completed) stories, I could always find something about them that needed more work. Fear of not being good enough at writing completely derailed me.

Well, courage might be the opposite of fear, but courage

isn't quite the linebacker I'd send out to tackle this issue.

Nope. This is a job for Confidence.

Lack of confidence, or loss of belief in oneself, or low self-esteem are all pretty much at the top of the list when it comes to struggles that creative people suffer from.

Ironically, most people don't suffer from this creative block until after they've seen rejection or failure a few times.

I'm inclined to believe that if we creatives do the inner work on our esteem **before seeking acceptance or approval from a subjective audience**, then we would have the opportunity to strengthen in preparation for the onslaught. Then, self-belief may take a hit but it probably wouldn't collapse.

A large part of our inner work is about confidence, either learning how to build it or figuring out how to get it back. Working on your confidence before you put yourself and your creative life out there for others to review is a mighty good idea.

However, if you're already out there, with flailing confidence, it's not too late to assess your natural creative forces and get your self-belief in tip-top shape.

When you assessed your natural creative forces back in chapter two, what came up for you in regard to confidence? Did it show up in any of those categories? In what way? Is this an area you need extra help with?

The most important benefit of confidence is creative flow. With flow comes acceptance, abundance, faith that you have the capability to learn, recognition of your value, and recognition of your power.

What you don't want to see happening is forced creativity, because then you're in a state of non-acceptance, fear, doubt, lack, and limiting beliefs.

Lack of Confidence Leads to Forced Creativity

Forcing your creativity takes you out of your power. You're approaching your work with the attitude that there is no other way you can make this happen, so you create in a place of fear.

Confident creatives don't need to force themselves to do their work. Their creative and real-world selves are so aligned that things flow at a natural state. Their energy is one of receiving, openness, and faith.

The state from which you take action creates the state of your mindset during the action. So if you're feeling inspired when you take action, you'll be in an inspired mindset during the action. This is your creative flow. You get to choose if you want it to be of the inspired variety or doubtful.

That's why getting yourself into the proper creativity mindset before you begin your project is so helpful! Taking just a few minutes to get into the best headspace for the project in question makes a big difference in your overall outcome.

Confidence is built from knowledge and tools already inside you, which means we all have the capability of living and creating confidently. Playing it safe and staying within the confines of your comfort zone will only allow you to be confident within that place. Stepping outside your self-imposed container and taking some risks is necessary for growth, creative or otherwise. Growth breeds confidence.

Go ahead and play in the sandbox of inspiration and ideas. That's the best place to start. And when you're ready, begin turning the sand into castles.

Act on the heels of your dreams. The life you truly desire lies outside your comfort zone.

WHERE CAN YOU MAKE THE CHANGE?

As I write this, our world is under orders to stay at home due to a deadly virus, Covid-19. To date, we've been in lockdown for over sixty days. For most people, life has changed drastically. Children are homeschooled. Many people are out of work. People are getting sick and dying at an alarming rate. Countries have closed their borders. Grocery stores are rationing toilet paper, pasta, and hand sanitizer.

Before I continue, I want to extend my prayers to everyone who was impacted by this terrible virus. I actually debated over including this topic in this book because I don't want to make light of the tragic outcomes so many people endured by focusing on suffering creativity.

Truth be told, though, this is a real moral dilemma for many people who never got sick, whose family members and friends didn't get sick, and who didn't lose jobs. The worst personal struggle they experience is the repetition and claustrophobic conditions of staying safe at home. Then there are those who complain of boredom, or that the virus isn't "real." Such complaints are callous and insensitive to those people who are on the front lines or who have lost loved ones to the virus.

I want to be clear that suffering creativity during this time is low on the totem pole of problems, yet this worldwide pandemic serves as a valuable lesson to creatives with a faulty or negative mindset.

Many people are finding themselves to be unmotivated during this time. Many are falling behind on their goals. The complaint of "no creativity" is a common theme on all social media platforms.

Interestingly, the reasons that most people aren't keeping up with their creative pursuits isn't because their schedules are wonky or that they've gotten sick or lost jobs—it's because they simply chose not to create.

There is no judgment here. Even though I'm a creative who is accustomed to working from home and my schedule is affected minimally, I'm not immune to the deep desire to cuddle with my cats on the couch and binge watch Netflix and hope the world fixes itself while I'm away.

I can feel the difference in the air between life before the virus and life after the virus. The realities of what we're facing are scary. Working on a novel or a blog post just doesn't seem all that important in the grand scheme of things.

And yet I don't choose Netflix and the cats. I continue working, like I've always done, and I continue to set daily and weekly goals, like I've always done. And truth be told, it's easy for me to choose my creative work.

I know why I'm able to show up without missing a beat. It's because I'm clear on why I need to create. It's because I'm confident in my creative journey. It's because, back when I restructured my inner landscape, I had established a set of ground rules for myself regarding my creative life. Part of that was deciding what I'd do when faced with extreme circumstances.

Covid-19 is an extreme circumstance and guess where I am?

During this time of lockdown and uncertainty, I'm answering the call to show up for people and to be a voice of support and compassion. I'm pouring my fear and anxiety and sadness into creative work. So far, I built an online course, created a deck of affirmation cards *(Positively Creative Affirmation Cards)*, am writing this book, and holding challenges for my peeps in my writing group. I'm in the process of clearing out years' worth of storm debris from my backyard (#QuarantineMission). I also picked up animation (an old hobby of mine) and I'm devouring books.

Basically, I suited up and showed up in areas where I felt I could make a difference, not just for my own well-being, but for anyone whose life I could touch.

No one has the power to shift the quarantine out of our lives. No one has the power to disarm the virus and send it packing (at least, not until scientists can come up with a vaccine). So what power do you have? Where can you find the power to make the change you seek? (These questions serve you not just during this global pandemic, but they serve you in any moment you lack motivation.)

The power is in YOU. You have the power to find solutions to problems.

Only you can decide how to handle your personal situation. If you feel angry or frustrated, then rant, vent, explode if you must. If you feel overwhelmed, then take a break. Absolutely be in touch with those emotions. But…if those emotions have so much hold over you that you can't complete Project A or Obligation B or Responsibility C, then you've lost touch with your power.

Once you hook into the power within you, and you seek solutions, your confidence will bloom. You're taking control, you're figuring things out, and you're making a change in your life. Confidence can only grow from those action steps.

Once Upon a Time

We all have a story (or several) we tell ourselves that doesn't serve us. It's part of our old programming that has set us up to believe things that aren't true. These stories are so ingrained in us that we often don't even know they're a part of our belief system. Many times we think we believe that thing because that's just the way it is.

Not until we start unpacking some heavy bags do we begin to understand we've kept ourselves down, blocked ourselves, and limited ourselves—all based on bad programming.

Try this journaling exercise to see in what ways you might be letting your story take away your power:

1. What is the story I've been telling myself about why I can't have/do what I want?
2. What do I believe is supporting this story? What are my beliefs surrounding this story I tell myself?
3. How can I reframe this so I feel good about myself and my situation?

It's human nature to blame external factors for personal struggles. However, when we focus our attention on those things we can't control, then our creative and real-world selves can't stay in alignment. Alignment happens when we focus on our power. What action can I take that will serve me or others for the highest good? If we're out of alignment, we lack clarity on problem-solving.

Tapping into your natural creative forces will help you get your creative and real-world selves in sync. This will foster the creative flow of inspiration and ideas and problem solving.

OPEN TO RECEIVE

To receive anything, you must be open and accepting. This means you must stand in your worth. If you're running a business and trying to attract new clients, you'll be more effective if you one hundred percent believe that you deserve the new clients, that you're worthy of the new clients, and that you'll be able to serve them for their highest good.

Yup, this means you gotta break out some good ol' confidence.

When you're in this mindset, your creative success will grow in proportion to how well you receive. You must believe that you're ready for this growth, and that you'll seize whatever opportunities come your way.

Journal through the following considerations:

1. How are you with boundaries around your space?
    Do you set them and stick to them?
2. How are you with boundaries around your time?
    Do you set them and stick to them?
3. How are you with boundaries around your energy?
    Do you set them and stick to them?
4. Do you let people interrupt you?

5. Are you a people-pleaser and sacrifice your goals for others?
6. Do you like how you're treated by others?
7. Do you ask for help?
8. Can you recognize your yellow flags of distress when they start to fly? (Overwhelm, stress, anxiety, annoyance.)

These emotions and others like it are blocks to receiving. In these moments, ask yourself, "How can I remove this block so I can be more open to receive?"

Can you surrender emotions or feelings from events of the past?

Creativity is a natural part of us, and we need to feed it readily and regularly for it to thrive. If we focus on what isn't working or stay stuck in the stuff that happened a day ago, then we can't also access fresh, flowing creativity.

When you hang out in a state of creativity more often, then you'll create more often. You'll be open to receiving inspiration and ideas and clients and whatever else you want, and confidence will grow.

Embrace Where You Are

Too often, we compare ourselves to the girl-next-door-on Instagram and we feel lousy about our progress. Seeing her wild success and happiness gets you wondering if you'll ever reach your own goals.

First, remember there is no such thing as an overnight success. You don't know what action steps the other person had to take to get to where they are. You're falling into the trap of comparing your messy prep area in the kitchen to someone's beautifully presented gourmet meal.

Second, you don't know what resources, time, and support they have available.

Third—and this is a major one—you don't know what their mindset was before, during, and after they reached their goals.

Half of success is taking action on the things you know and learn. The other half of success is believing in yourself as you take action.

Before you can be successful, you have to learn the ropes. You have to know stuff. Take classes, workshops, study, ask for help, get feedback. This takes time, energy, money, support, self-discipline, patience, and a little bit of ferocity. It will take as long as you need it to take. No more, no less.

However, remember that half of success is related to self-belief, aka, confidence? If you strengthen your mindset and do some "inner work," then you can speed up the learning process and get to your destination more swiftly and with more joy.

Understand that creativity, in all forms, takes time. Where you are now isn't where you were last month. You're closer to your goal through whatever actions you took. This is why tracking your progress is really helpful, because you can pinpoint your milestones and gauge which conditions are favorable for your growth.

For every moment you have doubt or worry, first, breathe, then assess your current position. Ask yourself if you can make a change then and there. What can you do differently that will help get you moving forward?

Make a choice—don't just wonder. Make a decision and

act on it. Above all, whatever choice you make, embrace it. Own it. Follow it through and see where it takes you. Then, assess again.

Celebrate Your Wins

Where you are today is based on the actions you took in the past. You got yourself to this moment. Every lesson you've learned has helped you grow and strengthen. What you do tomorrow, next week, and next month—all of that will move you toward your destination. Every action step you take counts. Every result matters.

Do you celebrate your progress? Do you congratulate yourself on a job well done? Do you reward yourself with pizza or a night out with friends or a day at the beach? Are you proud of yourself for even trying, or making an effort?

This is like a Jedi-mindset trick. By filling up on positive thoughts and compliments and beautiful self-care, we're attracting more positive mojo into our lives. When we're kind and supportive to ourselves, when we celebrate our wins, we'll find that kindness and support and more wins flow into our lives in unexpected and beautiful ways.

Ways to create wins
~ Step out of your comfort zone.
~ Act on your strengths and values.
~ Make a point of failing.
~ Believe in yourself.
~ Be open to learning and growth and receiving.
~ Give back to your community.
~ Take an action (bonus points for taking an action on something you've been putting off or avoiding).

"Making things happen in your life requires a faith, or an ability to believe that is unshakable, regardless of your circumstances."

LES BROWN

Chapter 8

KEEPING THAT STAR IN SIGHT

The best, and dare I say, most fun approach to hitching our wagon to a star is to establish and maintain positive creativity vibes. If you can get to the point where you're waking up each morning excited to spend time on your creative project, then you're fast-tracking through win after win after win. This is success in and of itself, and as long as you keep it up, that success will keep expanding and building into higher and higher levels of success.

But you have to get your positive mojo in tip-top shape first. Following is a small list of simple but powerful mindfulness tools that anyone can use.

It isn't necessary to do them all—unless you want to! Pick the ones that resonate with you the most, and then start building them into your daily schedule.

Let's hop to it.

Emotional Freedom Technique

Emotional Freedom Technique (EFT) or "Tapping" is an amazing self-help tool that you can do anywhere, anytime. It's like acupuncture without the needles. While you can practice EFT on your own and get amazing results, you can also consult licensed professionals to help you find "emotional freedom." To get yourself started, check out the many free YouTube videos available to help guide you through this amazingly simple yet powerful mental- and physical-clearing process.

One of my favorite tapping gurus is Brad Yates. I can't praise him enough. I learned about the concept of tapping through Gabby Bernstein, but it was Brad Yates who helped me develop a deeper understanding and appreciation of EFT and how to apply it in my life. (Learn more about Brad Yates on his website, Tap with Brad: https://tapwithbrad.mykajabi.com/.)

Tapping serves me best first thing in the morning, before I do anything else, and any time I'm under acute stress. The combination of speaking to myself and the physical movement is a wonderful precursor to meditation because it helps me to shake off any restlessness or anxiety—it calms my "monkey mind." Tapping clears out any cobwebs or devilish thoughts, which then allows meditation to work more effectively for me.

Meditation

I suffered from a series of panic attacks throughout my thirties. After what felt like the thousandth attack, I began to realize the only thing that helped me get through was focused breathing. And when I say "focused" I mean tuned in, centered on, close attention, to my breath. The timing of it. How it felt going through my body. What my breathing sounded like. With this focus, my thoughts simmered down and my body relaxed and the images in my head softened.

I remember wondering at one point if I was meditating. I wasn't sitting lotus style or humming. No incense or pillows. Just me, on the cold bathroom floor, in the fetal position. And yet, focused breathing was making me feel tons better.

These days we're taught to reach for external solutions for internal problems. While there are serious psychological and medical issues that require help from a professional, there are illnesses and ailments that can be overcome metaphysically.

Most of my life I suffered from anxiety and depression that seems to run in the family. We laughingly call it "the family depression," but in truth, there's nothing funny about it.

For whatever reason, no one spoke about solutions such as meditation. I try not to think about how many years I've spent battling my unhappiness and dissatisfaction with life—blaming myself, getting down on myself. When I found meditation, the veil lifted.

I'm not an expert on meditation at all. I highly encourage you to do your own research if you're interested in learning technique. What I can tell you is that the reason it works so well is because there's ultimate power in the "now." When we still our minds and focus on our breath (which is a beautiful rhythm), then we're hovering gracefully in the "now." Whatever "what if" or "but I can't" or "I should have" that had gripped us earlier is loosened and falls away. No, it doesn't just vanish. But it no longer holds us captive. *We see a glimpse of our power—power directly within us—and it's mightier than any fear or worry.*

Stop to think about that for a moment. We see a glimpse of our power—power directly within us—and it's mightier than any fear or worry. If we work to harness that power, to be able to find control over our minds/thoughts, and subsequently, our lives—just imagine the possibilities. Suddenly, making time to create or building a business doesn't sound so out of reach, does it?

Affirmations

As you know by now, I'm a big believer in affirmations. Repeating an affirmation over and over and over—even just one—can help to calm or pivot you out of negative self-talk.

I have different sets of affirmations that I use throughout the day depending on the situation at hand. Some help me start my day. Some I use in my pre-writing ritual. Some I use when my Inner Critic pipes up.

The following are generic affirmations that anyone can use and modify to fit their specific situation:

~ I'm a good writer.

~ I enjoy my creative time.

~ I love the art I'm creating.

~ I'm learning more and more every day.

~ My business is improving and strengthening.

If you're at such a low point in your creativity mindset that the above statements don't quite resonate, then modify them as such:

~ I'm learning how to become a good writer.
~ I'm eager to enjoy my creative time.
~ I'm becoming more excited about the art I'm creating.
~ Today I embrace the opportunity to learn and grow.

Why do affirmations work? Well, anything we tell ourselves we believe. So positive affirmations are as (if not more so) powerful and believable as self-criticism. Choose your self-talk carefully.

Old programming and old stories can be triggered without warning. If we're not careful, our minds will respond to those fears and limiting beliefs with negative chatter:

~ I'm not good enough.
~ I'm an outsider.
~ My art sucks.
~ No one believes in me.
~ I'm a fool for thinking I could run a business.

How often have you caught yourself on the Negative Train Loop? How long were you on this loop? Minutes? Hours? Days? How easy was it for you to jump off and get on a kinder train heading for a kinder destination?

At first, it probably wasn't easy—if you were able to jump off at all. Sometimes we don't have the self-awareness to make the jump ourselves, and we're stuck on these loops until something else comes along to redirect us.

The longer we're on these loops (I've been on them for days on end, and they're exhausting), the tougher it is to disengage.

That's why setting up a few go-to positive affirmations is key. Positive self-talk has as much power as negative self-talk, which means you have the power to change your mindset! We can teach ourselves to become aware of our thoughts, so that when we do get into the negative loops, we have a better chance of busting out of them.

But how do you even get started? How can you teach yourself to become aware of your thoughts? I'm sure there are many ways, but I can share with you how I did it and maybe it will work for you too.

First, I established a set of positive thoughts. They spanned several areas of my life including health, family, creativity, finances, where I live, my business, etc. Once I settled on a series of thoughts that made me feel good about myself, I added them to my phone.

I set twelve alerts on my phone at various times throughout the day, depending on my schedule. Some hours I had to skip because I knew I'd be driving or I'd be working with a client or something. I wanted to be available to see the alert and respond with gratitude when it came through, so that's why specific times were important for me.

As an example, at 11:11 every day I had an alert go off with the message *I am worthy*.

In fact, as this was a major pain point for me, this message was set for three separate times every day.

Other messages included:

~ I'm a great mom.

~ I'm blessed with a beautiful family.

~ Today is a beautiful day!

~ I'm building a business I'm proud of.

Each time the alert sounded, I would reach for my phone and see the message. I made a point of reciting it out loud (speaking the affirmations is hugely magical), I'd feel grateful for the thought, and I'd do a victory dance when I was reciting it because dancing raises our vibration.

It's fun, actually, especially in the beginning, because I hadn't yet acclimated to this new ritual, and I always felt surprised to get the alerts with these beautiful messages.

As the weeks wore on, the messages became firmly established as part of my belief system. I leveled-up the affirmations with stronger, feistier language.

I strengthened my belief system because I began to say the affirmations even when I wasn't being reminded by my phone. Anytime I had a few free minutes, like refreshing my coffee or putting the dog outside, a variety of affirmations were cycling through my head like they were in the Tour de France.

Ain't much room for negative self-talk when your mind is crammed with thoughts made of sugar and spice and everything nice.

VISUALIZATION

Creative visualization is like daydreaming on steroids. This particular personal development tool is the easiest for me because I daydreamed my way through childhood, adolescence, and most of my twenties. It's the primary reason I didn't do so hot in school.

Looking back, I wish I'd known that daydreaming, when applied with intention, can actually manifest into form.

"Thoughts become things" is a popular phrase that has been attributed to several people, although Mike Dooley is credited with the following modification: "Thoughts become things...choose the good ones!" It means what we think is our reality, so be smart about it. So if you start thinking about things you want to be true, rather than about things that already are true, you'll start to shift your reality. This is a huge mindset game changer.

If you can incorporate this kind of thought-maintenance in your life every day, you will feel brighter and lighter simply because your head is filled with good-feeling mojo, not crap.

If you want to know more about this practice of mental imagery, I highly recommend Shakti Gawain's book, *Creative Visualization*.

The trick with creative visualization is that you need to feel the feels when you're imagining the life of your dreams. It helps to be someplace quiet where you can't be disturbed, so I find doing this first thing in the morning or right before I go to bed are two great times.

In terms of supporting our creativity mindset, visualization can help us find our "happy place." If we conjure a scene in our minds where we're sitting in our workspaces, happily producing the stuff of our dreams, and allow ourselves to feel the emotion of that future self we've conjured, then we're actively raising our vibration.

The other trick I should mention is we need to remove resistance or doubt from our visualizations. If this feels too difficult, then start small, with a desire that feels doable and within the realm of possibility. Then you can work your way up to bigger, fancier desires.

Here are some examples of how visualization can help you manifest or improve your creative workspace:

~ Draw a picture of your ideal workspace, if you don't have one yet. Mark all the places where you would keep your tools and equipment.

Hang your drawing someplace where you can see it daily, or add it into your journal. Add to it anytime a new idea occurs.

Every morning take a look at your drawing, and then spend fifteen minutes visualizing yourself in this space. Let yourself get excited. See yourself sitting at your desk, smiling as you speak to a client on the phone, or opening up your emails to find a business offer. Picture yourself working on the project of your dreams and it's going well. Allow those feelings of excitement and happiness to surge through you.

~ If you already have a workspace, take a photo of it in its most efficient and organized state and tack that photo in a space where you can see it daily. This is your motivation to use it to its fullest potential. Picture yourself making amazing business deals from this workspace.

~ Write in your journal about A Day in the Life (in your most ideal creative workspace). Pretend you're recapping what it's like to have the creative sanctuary of your dreams, what kinds of tasks you do, how it's decorated, what it smells like, what sounds you can hear if you open the window or door.

The above techniques are great kick-off points for any area of your life. Spend a weekend making a vision board filled with pictures and words that represent the ideal future you. You can use that vision board as part of your visualization practice.

Journaling/Scripting

Journaling through your dreams, fears, goals, and blocks will help you create a positive creativity mindset. Your journal is your ultimate safe place, where you can feel free to vent, wish, rage, and aspire.

Some people shy away when I mention the word "journal," and I wonder if it's because they think I'm talking about jotting down your deepest, darkest thoughts. While journals are great spaces for that, I'm thinking of using a journal in terms of tracking your progress—with anything.

For example, if you're trying to achieve a productivity goal with your business, try tracking it in a journal. I love writing out a goal, then working backwards through the steps to get to where I am currently, and then examining not only my concrete progress from day-to-day, but also my mental/emotional states. Daily check-ins that include mood-monitoring and happiness-o-meters are amazing mindset reports that help me ditch strategies that aren't working and look for other options.

Journals can be used as time-keepers as well. You can keep track of how long it takes you to complete a certain task over the course of a week, two weeks, a month, and more—and along the way indicate the factors that may have impeded your productivity or enhanced it.

Another lovely use for a journal is scripting. This mindset practice involves writing down in detail a certain vision or dream you'd like to make come true. Similar to visualization, scripting leads you straight to the heart of the event and encourages you to feel emotion while you're writing down the experience.

The trick to successful scripting is to write in the present tense or past tense—not future. You want to write as though the event has already taken place or that it's currently unfolding. Bring in all the senses—smells, sounds, tastes, textures, and sights—to make it surge with realness. Allow your emotions to rise along with the vision as if it really is happening.

And of course, you can use journaling for . . . well, journaling! One of the best ways to clear out stuff weighing on your mind is to write it all out as a form of release. In regard to journaling about your creative life, think in terms of your natural creative forces and ask yourself some questions to be sure you aren't going easy on yourself by only skimming the surface.

Everyone has a dossier of traits, values, struggles, habits, strengths, challenges, motivations, beliefs, moods, and desires that work for and against them in their creative quest. Do you know what works for you? What bad habits can't you shake? What vision is driving you forward with determination?

Exploring your personal system of natural creative forces

will help you get to the root of any issues. Journaling over the course of just a few days will help you learn which aspects of your natural creative forces benefit your momentum and energy. This is a huge bonus when trying to build a positive creativity mindset practice.

Oracle/Tarot Cards

Card reading is gaining more and more popularity as the world we live in veers more toward listening to our voices within.

Success with card reading comes with trusting our intuition—and tuning out our logical minds.

All these mindfulness tools require some practice in order to gain confidence, but I'd say in general, card reading is the most difficult of them all.

One preliminary step to take before reading cards is to ground yourself. Grounding is simply a way to help you relax and center yourself, tuning out the external noise and tuning into your intuition. Grounding will help you become a clear channel for the intuitive messages you're meant to hear.

Card reading can help you tap into your creative power for the day. Once you learn how to distinguish your intuition from your ego, then you can ask specific questions about anything you want to get clarity on. For creatives, this is truly helpful in that we can get guidance on various projects, clients, or business decisions.

To ground yourself, simply sit in a quiet, comfortable space, placing your feet on the ground. Close your eyes and imagine roots traveling from your feet and into the earth.

Picture yourself drawing the earth's energy back up through the roots, into your feet, and through your whole body. Sink into the feeling of connection to Mother Earth, which, obviously, is grounding energy.

As Mother Earth's energy fills you up, it pushes out any negative energy that doesn't serve you. Imagine that unhelpful energy draining from your body, into the earth, where it will be transmuted. Breathe deeply and calmly while you perform this technique. Spend as much or as little time as you want until you're feeling centered.

Now you're ready to pull cards. There are many different rituals and methods involving the shuffling and selecting of cards. If this is something you're interested in learning further, I suggest researching Colette Baron-Reid, Denise Linn, or Brigit Esselmont. You can learn some basic strategies and from there formulate a practice that is personal to you.

Crystals

Just like everything else on this planet, crystals hold energy, but due to their perfect atomic symmetry crystals are powerful transmitters of vibration. This is why people can tap into their energy for healing, manifesting, wellness, protection, talismans, and guidance.

Crystals can be used in your mindset practice to create positive change. Each crystal has its own special "ability" or remedy to help you overcome a particular block, or to help promote or foster a strength in any area of your life.

Not only do I find great healing vibes through crystals, but also through rocks, shells, moss, driftwood, and other natural treasures I come across when I'm exploring nature.

It's difficult for me to go into a forest or walk along a beach without finding something to tuck into my pocket.

In fact, stones or other natural items that come from places special to us, like our backyard or a favorite beach, will carry meaningful energy for us. So if you're hesitant to invest in a crystal collection, why not start with interesting finds around your favorite stomping grounds?

Gratitude

This method is, hands down, undeniably fail-proof. You can't go wrong with it. In theory, feeling gratitude might seem simplistic or self-defeatist—especially when we're trying to improve our life. Why do we want to thank the Universe if we're not feeling red-hot about how things are going?

The Universe picks up on and responds with energy. Like attracts like, remember? So if you're spending your day feeling grumpy, and you notice that your day is only going downhill—have you ever thought "How can things get any worse?"—well, things are going downhill. That's the vibration you're putting out into the Universe, and it's responding in kind.

Gratitude works just like positive affirmations—thinking about things that make you happy, that light you up, that get your heart racing, or that simply fill you with peace conjure a joyful energy that will be reflected back to you.

A fun game I like to play is Gratitude Minute. Try to think of as many things you're thankful for in one minute. Another technique is to give yourself a category, say, Family, and write down everything you can think of that you're thankful for in regard to family.

I keep a Gratitude Journal and every night before bed I write down four pages worth of things I'm thankful for: my feather pillows, songbirds, pizza, movie night, indoor plumbing, cream in my coffee, my backyard fox, my clients, a day of writing—whatever comes to mind. Then I write a Letter of Magic, a full-page letter to the Universe thanking it for things I don't yet have, but I'm writing as though I do have them.

Feeling grateful for what you have reminds you that you're responsible for bringing those things into your life. Our lives are so chock-full and busy that we tend to take for granted we have food in our fridges or trees in our yards or friends we can call. Focus on what is working and thriving in your life, and you'll be able to conjure more of the things you want.

How to Put These Mindfulness Tools to Use

One or a combination of the above tools can be used to help boost your creativity mindset. You may want to create a ritual that incorporates any of the methods and use it to help kickstart your day, re-energize you midday, or ease you into a peaceful night's sleep.

Incense, candles, music, pillows, essential oils, tea, or water to drink are some examples of sensory details you can add to your experience.

When I began to develop a ritual, I knew it made sense to set one for first thing in the morning because I tend to pack in a lot in the AM hours. I also knew that later in the day I'm vulnerable to limiting beliefs because I'm tired or stressed, so incorporating a second ritual mid-afternoon would be a helpful pick-me-up.

I like to mix and match various methods depending on what's going on for the day. Some mornings I'm energetic and not weighed down by leftover thoughts from the day before, so I might skip tapping. On mornings with gorgeous weather and light, I often go out to my porch or backyard and dive right into visualization, scripting, and meditation. Other mornings when I'm feeling heavy, I'll likely do a combo of tapping, meditation, card pulls, and scripting!

For me, tapping is a technique that helps clear out the gunk. Meditation is a tool that centers and calms me. Affirmations, gratitude, crystals, and pulling cards are guidance systems that point me in the right direction—toward self-love, worthiness, and inner strength. Visualization is a method that reinforces my dreams and desires through imagery and emotion. Scripting is an exercise in my co-creation with the Universe.

They all have their own special magic, and because they all work for our highest good, one isn't better than another. Try out whichever one calls to you and develop your own personal ritual that can help strengthen your positive creativity mindset.

*"A creative life is an amplified life.
It's a bigger life, a happier life, an expanded life,
and a hell of a lot more interesting life."*

ELIZABETH GILBERT

Chapter 9

HONORING YOUR CREATIVITY

At the start of every day, you have a choice to either follow through on your commitment to your creative journey, or to take a detour. This is a choice you have every single day. No one gets to make it for you. And if you try to get out of this responsibility by claiming you have no time or you're interrupted too often, then you have relinquished some of your power.

Make no mistake, I don't deny that committing to a creative journey can be extremely difficult and stressful. But if we're complaining, making excuses, or letting ourselves get taken down without redesigning our schedules, re-envisioning, or breaking bad habits, then we are the ones creating our own struggle.

Are You a Creative in Your Mind?

If you don't think you're an artist, entrepreneur, writer, musician, or singer then you won't act like one.

Decide who you want to be.

And don't just stop at "I'm a photographer." What kind of photographer? What are your crazy-good skills? What's your favorite part about being a photographer? What kinds of things do you want to accomplish with your photography? How do you want to serve others for their highest good with your creative work?

Next, ask yourself about your values.

How do your values play into your creative work? What would you like to be able to do with your creative work that will align with your values? What about your values can you act upon now? What might take more time, education, or skills?

Be careful as you start to tread into areas where things might feel like they aren't working. If you focus on where you're struggling, then that's what you'll see all around you. Anything that's working or blossoming will become invisible or won't matter to you.

Limiting beliefs and negative perceptions will affect how you show up in the world. You'll suffer from a lack of clarity in your vision and doubt your destination. This will lead to an unclear journey. Let go of the beliefs that don't serve you.

You have to remember that there will always be an aspect of your creative journey that needs refining, but that's part of growth. If you have no more growing to do, then you've hit your ceiling, and things will get pretty darn boring! The other thing to always remember is that good things come out of fear and discomfort.

Rather than getting down on yourself for what you might perceive as limitations or failure, see them as opportunities.

Now, decide on reasonable goals and action steps that make you feel good.

Not easy, mind you. Good. Goals that raise your vibration and draw you to your creative journey. Action steps that fit with where you are currently.

If you're picking goals and action steps that aren't aligned with who you want to be, or that aren't aligned with the creative forces that serve you, then they won't matter enough or they'll be very difficult to achieve.

If your goals and action steps aren't reasonable (possible to achieve based on where you are in your journey), then you're setting yourself up for self-sabotage.

Your goals need to make sense according to the creative forces that serve you, and you need to take action steps that are aligned with where you are and what you know in your current circumstances.

Goal setting helps you grow in alignment with your highest vision, your truest self. Goal setting is one of the best strategies you can use to help you hitch your wagon to that star.

Finally, make a commitment to the creative that you decided you're going to be.

Decisions are easy once you make your commitment because of clarity. Write up a pledge. Draw that hard line in the sand:

~ I will promote my business every day.
~ I will eat a healthy meal.
~ I will write every morning.
~ I will learn something new today to build my business.
~ I will turn off social media so I can focus on my creative work.

There is no room for "Maybe I'll promote my business today. It depends on how my afternoon plays out." No, that just gives you freedom to not do the work. That allows you the choice to be wishy-washy. That allows you resistance and avoidance.

The million-dollar question: *What do I need to do to honor my creative self today?*

BREAKING A PROMISE TO YOURSELF

You might be frustrated or impatient or distressed that you aren't finding the success you were hoping for. A typical reaction is to change the goal. Before you change the goal, assess your action steps.

If you did the work necessary to determine what kind of a creative you want to be, then you should have decided upon clear, definitive goals that feel good to you. It may not be the goal that's the problem, but the path you're taking. Also, ask yourself if you're being impatient. Remember, growth is part of the journey. Are there things that need to fall into place first, before you can reach your destination?

Be mindful about changing your goals. Changing your goal because you outgrew the goal is one thing. Changing your goal because you can't hack it means that you're breaking a promise to yourself and you chip away at your self-confidence. That's why it's vital to have a clear mindset on who you are as a creative, what you want to accomplish in your creative life, and why it matters to you before you set forth on your journey.

Let's Review:

~ Decide who you want to be as a creative.

~ Understand and commit to your values.

~ Be sure your goals are reasonable and match your values.

~ Be sure your action steps make sense and are aligned with where you are and what you know in your current situation.

~ Align your path to the creative forces that serve you, and adjust when things aren't feeling good or healthy.

MISSION STATEMENTS FOR CREATIVES

In chapter four I suggested drawing up a creative spirit pledge to help you make a commitment to your new way of being, to celebrate the Creative You.

A mission statement differs in that it focuses on your "why," your reasons for wanting to hitch your wagon to that star.

Mission statements are excellent grounding techniques we can use to help us commit to what we do, who we want to engage, and why.

You can formulate your own mission statement to help you gain some clarity and confidence on your creative journey. Following is a breakdown of the steps you can take to help you get started.

What do I create?

Art? Music? Photography? Websites? Books? Businesses? Workshops or other teaching material? Blog posts? Gardens? Food?

What compels me to create?

Personal pleasure? Education? Raising awareness? Supporting others? Entertainment? Passion for the subject area?

You may find that there's more than one reason you create the things you do. That's normal, but you want to narrow it down to a common theme as much as possible so that your ultimate mission statement is clear and focused.

Who do I want to engage?

In other words, who is your audience? Think about gender, age, socioeconomic status, pain points, interests, traits, values, and beliefs.

Why do I create?

Return to the work you did in chapter two and review your thoughts and responses regarding your creative purpose. Compare those to how you answered the second question (what compels me to create) and see if common themes pop up.

Your purpose should be driven by your desires. In other words, if your purpose is to run a successful business that serves women, what compels you to do that work should be in some way aligned with your desire to help women. If there's a disconnect between these two areas, then you need to reassess.

CRAFT YOUR MISSION STATEMENT

Put your answers together from the previous questions, formulating a statement that feels good to you and one that reflects your vision and ideals.

How to live and create by your mission statement

Don't just write this down and never look at it again. This is a powerful affirmation to how you want to live and create from this day forward, so display it wherever it will bring you the most inspiration.

Make copies of it so that you can see it every day, under various circumstances. If you have a website, add it to your About Me page. Use it as a jumping point to write a journal entry. Turn it into one of your personal quotes and use it for branding purposes. Visit this statement anytime you're feeling a lack of clarity or motivation. Tack it on to a vision or dream board.

As you grow and evolve, it's likely that your mission statement will grow and evolve as well. Every once in a while, review the statement and refine it as necessary to reflect who you are today, who you want to engage today, and why.

HONORING YOUR CREATIVITY EVERY DAY

Building a positive creativity mindset takes practice. It's really a lifestyle. Every day, from the moment you wake up all the way through the moment you go to bed, you're given opportunities to be or not to be the best version of your creative self.

It's been said the average human has over 60,000 thoughts a day. That's at least 60,000 opportunities a day to live a joyful, abundant, and creative life. And the first thought of that 60,000 occurs the moment you wake up.

Do you know what you generally think about upon waking? How about your second thought? Fifth? What is your first action step after your alarm wakes you up? How about the second action step? The tenth?

Whatever you think and whatever you do in those moments that open your day set the tone for every moment following—unless you make a conscious effort to pivot.

Spend the next few days spying on yourself. Pay attention to your thoughts immediately upon waking. Track your action steps as closely as possible. Try to do a few thought check-ins throughout the day. Record your findings. Do not judge yourself for anything you learn. Simply observe, record, and release.

When you feel like you've found some patterns or habits that you'd like to address, ask yourself some questions:

1. What is my most common emotion when I wake up?
2. Why do I feel this way?
3. How do I manage this emotion?
4. What is my overriding emotion throughout my morning? Afternoon? Evening?
5. At what point in my day do I honor my creativity? Is this satisfactory to me? Why?
6. What thoughts would I like to change?

7. What new thoughts will replace those?
8. With my new thoughts as part of my daily practice, how will I honor my creativity every day?

At this point, you're restructuring your mindset. You're targeting the negative thoughts and finding new ones that support your greatest desires. With this new foundation of positive thinking, you can begin building a joyful, creative life.

As you evolve, your practice will likely need to evolve. You'll know whether your daily practice is calibrated to the specific needs of your long-term vision through regular journey checks:

1. What did I do today that brought me joy?
2. In what way did I give back today?
3. What did I say or do today that's in alignment with my core values?
4. If today was less than wonderful, how did I treat myself or others?
5. What did I say or do today that's meaningful?
6. What did I nurture today?
7. How do I feel about my long-term vision?

Stand Up for Your Creative Journey

Feeling good and positive about your creative journey starts with YOU. We like to listen far too much to people who have negative things to say, as if embracing limiting beliefs protects us or prepares us for a potential negative outcome.

Does that really make sense? You spend your journey

hiding from a fear that may or may not happen? What kind of lessons and growth do you think you'll encounter in that state of being?

Take back your power and tap into your creative spirit. What is it you want in your life? Who do you want to be on your journey? Are you ready to be a high-vibing creative? Maybe you're just getting started or maybe you're thinking it's time to level up your practice. Wherever you are in your journey, know that a joyful, creative life is yours for the taking. Your creative spirit is always ready to fill you with inspiration and joy.

Are you open to receiving?

Tip #1: Know your natural creative forces.

If you don't know under what conditions you work best, then you need to figure that out as soon as possible. Routines always hinge on actions and reactions, and the most successful routines align with your strengths and high energetic zones.

Tip #2: Set boundaries.

Guard your mindset practices. If you live with other people, make sure they understand you aren't to be disturbed when you're doing this inner work. You may get some pushback, so it's important you're clear and firm. Explain why this work is important and how you expect it will serve you—not just in your creative life but all aspects of your life. Don't forget—it isn't just other people who can mess with your practice. Pay attention to where you might self-sabotage and hold yourself back, and get tough on yourself when you do.

Tip #3: KISS

Keep It Sweet & Simple. Aligning with your creative spirit should be fun and enjoyable. If you make your mindset practice too complex you'll have a harder time sticking with it. To start, pick one or two mindfulness tools from chapter eight that appeal to you most. Establish those before you add on anything else. Assess your progress from week to week and don't be afraid of swapping out some methods for others until you find the perfect blend for you.

Tip #4: Want it.

We can make anything happen if we want it badly enough. No one is saying it'll be easy or that you'll find success overnight. But you'll get a win every time you show up. When the wins start piling up, not only will you be closer to your dream, but you'll feel different. More energized. More confident. More courageous. But to get there you have to want it badly enough that you'll push through the obstacles and learn the lessons.

Tip #5 Clarify Your Purpose

Knowing your purpose and understanding WHY you're doing any of this work is hugely helpful in establishing a mindset practice. Even if it's simply to find personal stability in a chaotic world, as long as it's an important outcome or result to you, then that will be your driving force.

Tip #6 Take Marvelous Care of Yourself

Self-care is critical in the maintenance of your creativity mindset. If you don't take care of yourself, then it'll be difficult to do the inner work that's needed for a strong, healthy, positive creative life.

Everyone will need to design their own self-care routine that works best for them. Where one person may need to focus more on adequate sleep, another person may need to pay attention to physical exercise.

Regardless of your special circumstances, keep in mind that all elements that make up YOU are important in their own way. Sleep may come easily to you, but that could be because you don't watch television before bed. If you aren't aware of why you sleep well, then it's easy to introduce a habit that could disturb your sleep patterns. This is true for all areas of self-care, which is another reason why understanding your natural creative forces is so important.

Tip #7 You are Worthy

You have to believe that you're worthy of following your creative dreams. You're worthy of that star, so go get your wagon and hitch it up. The dreams you have are yours for a reason. You have every right to them. Some will be easy to snag, while others will take some work, requiring more growth from you. The raw beauty of dreams is in the discovery, the adventuring, and the creating. Embrace the journey and believe you're worthy of having anything you desire.

JOYFULLY EVER AFTER

A creative journey that is meaningful and fulfilling and authentic is a long road. There will be days where you might want to take a break even after you've set goals and made commitments. It's okay. There's nothing wrong with taking time for yourself, and when you do I want you to

Be gentle with yourself. Breathe in. Breathe out. Relax. Soften the lights. Sit in water. Eat sweet fruit. Take a nap. Embrace the now. Soak in the sunrise. Feed the birds. Play music that makes you move. Watch a movie that makes you smile. Talk to a friend who makes you laugh. Read a book that makes you think. Write down thoughts that make you grow. Be kind. Listen to your inner child. Breathe in. Breathe out. Rest in the shade of a tree. Add magic. Wonder. Forgive yourself. Collect seashells. Allow. Be wild. Be happy. Be free. Have faith. Try again. Believe in yourself. Wear slippers. Give out hugs. Breathe in. Breathe out. Play with puppies. Drink fresh, clean water. Put your heart to good use. Be curious. Create with abandon. Make time for loved ones. Make time for you.

And when you're ready, hitch your wagon right back up. Your positively creative journey is waiting for you.

Acknowledgements

I wrote this book to empower creatives so they can hitch their wagons to their dream-stars. Creativity is a living, breathing force within each one of us, and we have the power to harness the magic in ways that bring adventure, beauty, and fulfillment to our daily lives.

The guidance inside these pages is meant to help you transform your limiting beliefs to a positive mindset for joyful creative living. A tall order like that calls for the support and wisdom of a team. I absolutely needed the help of some marvelous people to help me pull my ideas and thoughts into book form for the enjoyment of others.

Thank you so much, Alexa Bigwarfe. Your excitement and encouragement surrounding this book and my entire vision for providing inspiration and support to creatives helped me see the light at the end of the tunnel.

Thank you Michelle Fairbanks for your work on the cover design—you were so easy to work with from start to finish, and thank you Audrey Hodge for your skillful editing and quick turn-around.

Much love to my Team Writer community, who inspire me and challenge me daily to be the best writer and coach that I can be.

Shout-outs to all the people who have liked my posts, commented on my articles, continued the conversation, asked a question, worked with me, bought my books and courses, participated in my writing challenges and workshops, hired me for coaching or editing, and all-around supported me on this wild ride we call creativity. Each one of you is a guiding light for me and a big reason I keep showing up. Thank you so much.

Finally, this book would never have made it past the idea stage without the loving support and patience of my husband and children. I know it's hard for non-writers to truly understand or appreciate exactly what all is involved in turning a seed of a book idea into a book, full in bloom. I'm actually not altogether sure myself, but I can say without a doubt that the main ingredient is faith. They believed in me, which only nurtured the belief I have in myself. Love y'all to the moon and back.

About The Author

Kate Johnston is a writing coach, book editor, and author. Her clients range from budding writers to traditionally published authors. She specializes in mindset coaching to empower people to tap into their natural creative forces so they can attract the creative life they desire.

She is the creator of *Positively Creative Affirmation Cards*, a mindfulness tool designed to help you connect to and honor your creative spirit so that you can call upon your potential to achieve your greatest dreams.

When Kate isn't working with writers, or immersed in her own fiction, she's busy with Writers for Wildlife, a program she founded to raise funds for non-profit organizations worldwide to support their efforts in conservation protections and emergency relief.

Website:
katejohnstonauthor.com

Instagram:
instagram.com/katejauthor

Pinterest:
pinterest.com/katejauthor

Facebook Writing Group:
facebook.com/groups/TeamWriter

Author's Note

Thank you so much for your purchase of *Positively Creative*. Did you know that you just helped me support endangered species across the planet through my fundraising program Writers for Wildlife?

To learn more about the charities I support, check out Writers for Wildlife:
https://katejohnstonauthor.com/writers-for-wildlife/

I hope you enjoyed this book.
If you'd like to receive updates on future products and services, please contact Kate Johnston at:

Email: kate@katejohnstonauthor.com
Website: katejohnstonauthor.com

Recommended Resources

Below is a list of references that I highly recommend to help you further develop your creativity mindset practices.

Andrews, Ted. *Animal Speak: The Spiritual & Magical Powers of Creatures Great & Small.* Llewellyn Publications, 1993.

Bernstein, Gabrielle. *The Universe Has Your Back: Transform Fear to Faith.* Hay House, 2016.

Breathnach, Sarah Ban. *Simple Abundance: A Daybook of Comfort and Joy.* Warner Books, Inc. 1995.

Byrne, Rhonda. *The Secret.* Atria Books. 2006.

Gawain, Shakti. *Creative Visualization: Use the Power of Your Imagination to Create What You Want in Your Life.* New World Library, 2002.

Gilbert, Elizabeth. *Big Magic: Creative Living Beyond Fear.* Riverhead Books. 2015.

Hicks, Esther, and Jerry. *The Law of Attraction: The Basics of the Teachings of Abraham.* Hay House, 2006.

Salzberg, Sharon. *Real Happiness: The Power of Meditation.* Workman Publishing Company, Inc. 2011.

Van Doren, Yulia. *Crystals: The Modern Guide to Crystal Healing.* Quadrille Publishing Ltd. 2017.

www.ingramcontent.com/pod-product-compliance
Lightning Source LLC
Chambersburg PA
CBHW072019110526
44592CB00012B/1374